AN ORDINARY MAN DURING
THE EXTRAORDINARY TIME

To Cecil & ALL of your Family.

Your Friend,
Rosemary (Snider) Hunt

AN ORDINARY MAN DURING THE EXTRAORDINARY TIME

ROSEMARY GILDER

TATE PUBLISHING
AND ENTERPRISES, LLC

An Ordinary Man During The Extraordinary Time
Copyright © 2015 by Rosemary Gilder. All rights reserved.

No part of this publication may be reproduced, stored in a retrieval system or transmitted in any way by any means, electronic, mechanical, photocopy, recording or otherwise without the prior permission of the author except as provided by USA copyright law.

This book is designed to provide accurate and authoritative information with regard to the subject matter covered. This information is given with the understanding that neither the author nor Tate Publishing, LLC is engaged in rendering legal, professional advice. Since the details of your situation are fact dependent, you should additionally seek the services of a competent professional.

The opinions expressed by the author are not necessarily those of Tate Publishing, LLC.

Published by Tate Publishing & Enterprises, LLC
127 E. Trade Center Terrace | Mustang, Oklahoma 73064 USA
1.888.361.9473 | www.tatepublishing.com

Tate Publishing is committed to excellence in the publishing industry. The company reflects the philosophy established by the founders, based on Psalm 68:11,
"The Lord gave the word and great was the company of those who published it."

Book design copyright © 2015 by Tate Publishing, LLC. All rights reserved.
Cover design by Norlan Balazo
Interior design by Jomar Ouano

Published in the United States of America

ISBN: 978-1-68207-085-7
Biography & Autobiography / General
15.10.05

This is the true story of Art, who in 1910, at the end of eighth grade, his father made him quit school and go to work. Art worked in sawmills around Green Bay, Wisconsin, and in a steel mill down in Milwaukee. He then decided to hop a train to Montana to work in the wheat fields, but a drought caused him to change his course and go up to Moose Jaw, British Columbia, Canada, to find work up there. While in Moose Jaw, he injured his leg and has to stay at least six months for his leg to heal. He then hopped another train to Portland, Oregon. In Portland, he decided to ride a paddleboat up the Columbia River to The Dalles, Oregon. It was while he was working in The Dalles on a wheat ranch that he was drafted into WWI. While in boot camp, the war ended, and in September, he was honorably discharged from the service. Although he does not talk about it, he spends a few years up in Alaska, trapping fur-bearing animals and making enough money to buy a little farm in Parkdale, Oregon, located in the Hood River Valley of Oregon. This is just the first half of his young adventurous life. From 1927 to 1928, he and his girlfriend wrote letters back and forth to each other almost every day, capturing the everyday life of rural living. Throughout this story of a boy coming of age into adulthood is the story of a young United States and her coming of age at the turn of the century and into the late 1920s and her maturity.

Contents

Part 1: The Early Years

Turning 102 Years: 1999	11
Wisconsin and Timber: 1897	15
Sawmills	19
Strikes	23
The Steel Mills	25
Going Out West	31
Wheat Harvest in Canada	35
The Woolen Mill in Canada	39
The Columbia River and Oregon	41
My Experiences on a Wheat Ranch	45
Drafted into WWI	51
Mustering In	53

Part 2: Art and Elsie The Courtship Years: 1927–1928

Goldendale, Washington 57

Parkdale, Oregon 59

Hood River Strawberries 61

Boxing and the Radio 75

Dee Oregon 85

Bridge of the Gods and Charles Lindbergh....................... 95

Boxing and the 1920s 99

Joseph Cukoschay a.k.a. Jack Sharkey.............................. 101

Gene Tunney-The Fighting Machine............................... 103

Jack Dempsey 105

The Long Count Fight 107

1928.. 127

Plowing and Harrowing 137

Beacon Rock, Washington 151

Postscript 159

Rosemary Gilder's Bio 161

PART 1

The Early Years

Turning 102 Years: 1999

I was born in Marinette, Wisconsin, on January 5, 1897, and today, I turned 102 years old. I can't believe that I have lived to be 100, let alone to live to be 102. I wonder if I will make it to be 103. They asked me what I wished for as I blew out my three candles that spell out 102. What did I wish for? Oh. I wished that I could hold my dear sweet Elsie in my arms again. I missed her dearly. Although I married a second time, it was Elsie who was the love of my life. I waited a long time to find her, court her, and married her, and it seemed like a blink and she was gone. I missed her every day.

A young newspaper reporter came to the nursing home where I am now confined. She takes a lot of pictures and asked a bunch of questions. Foolhardy questions like, "What's it like to be 102 years old?" I wanted to say, "Well, what you think it's like?" but I just laugh and say, "Well, I don't righty know, I haven't given it much thought." But I have given it considerable thought, for that is all I do these days is remember my past and how old I am and how life has changed, not only for me but also for the United States of America.

The nursing staff makes a big fuss over birthdays for those of us living here, and on account of it being my birthday, it's my turn for that flurry of activity. One of which is this fool reporter who is quite determined to get a story out of me even if it kills me. You know, I never was one who wanted to have a fuss made over me. I want out of here, so I motioned for a CNA to come over. When she did, I whispered in her ear, "I want to go back to my room, could you take me?" She said, "Sure!" and away we rolled. She asked me if I wanted to lie down on my bed or sit in my wheelchair and look out the window. I chose the window so that I could look out at the snow falling on the bushes. As I was just settling in with my thoughts, there was a knock on my door, and the reporter quietly walks in and holds out her hand for a second introductory handshake. "Hello, Art. May I come in and ask you a few more questions to complete the article that I am writing. It's not every day that someone gets to turn 102 years." This newspaper reporter looks so young. How could she be interested in my story?

I am afraid that I am just a craggily looking old man. Even to me, I look old. I look at the mirror in the mornings and think who *is* this old man looking back at me? I don't recognize myself anymore. I remember that, at one time, I had been considered a decent-looking man, not that I'm bragging, it's just what I've been told. Back then, my smoky-blue eyes were offset by my short brown hair and a clean-shaven face. I never cared much for a beard or mustache, so I never had the desire to place either of them on my face.

I was not what you consider a tall man, but I never seemed to mind my five-foot-seven-inch frame. It seemed to suite me very well though it seems that the seven-inch part is shorter these days. I don't know if it's my age or all the hard work I have done in my life. Now mind you, I didn't mind all that hard work though being in the outdoors has put a permanent tan on my face and hands so that even today, it looks like I was just outside working all day. She repeats her questions, "How is it that you came from Wisconsin out to Oregon? And what was your favorite time period of your life?"

I told her, "The answer to your first question not only has to do with my life's history but also that of our nation's young history. Both histories are tied up within each other. The answer to your second question is when I was courting my dear sweet Elsie, and again, our courting histories were wrapped up with our nation's history. You see, we wrote to each other for almost two years, almost every day or every other day of the week. And when we weren't writing letters back and forth, I would go see her. Would you like to read my letters sometime?" She said that, indeed, she would love to read our letters if it was all right with me. But, of course, it is. I am warming up to this young woman who shows a deep respect and interest in my life's story. "Do you have time for me to tell you about my adventures west?" She poised her pen and said, "Yes, I do have time, and I really want to hear your stories." In order for any of my story to make sense, I have to tell her about my home state of Wisconsin and my hometown and the industries that shaped the landscapes and me as well.

Wisconsin and Timber: 1897

My home state of Wisconsin had a very colorful beginning. For 160 years, between the years of 1634 and 1794, Wisconsin was mostly populated by the many Indian tribes. Then later, the Jesuit missionaries, the French voyageur Jean Nicolet, and the French fur traders came. Wisconsin's timbers were rich in volume both in circumference and plentiful. After the traders, came the colonizers and the common everyday pilgrims. The trees were one of the most easily visible and accessible resources of the day. The vast forests supplied the wood for the buildings that would become the stores, homes, furniture, barns, fences, and buildings for schools, churches, and industries that would become settlements, towns, and later, cities. Each successive group of pioneers transformed the tangled wilderness of trees and brush into ordered civilianization.

In the densely wooded areas around the Atlantic seaboard and the trans-Appalachian country, the pioneers found that the forests not only supplied the necessities but also was a huge obstruction to progress. The pioneers had to do great battle with his ax and still, after two centuries of his mighty efforts, the pioneers still were not conquerors of the woods. As long as the paths of the settlements stayed close the forested areas, there was no extensive trade in lumber. The villagers got their lumber from primitive sawmills that sprang up in every community. This is why at the time of my youth, there were thirty-seven sawmills in and around my hometown of Marinette and neighboring towns. The mills around Marinette processed hardwood, Norway spruce, and white pine with power generated from hydroelectricity. It was only when the villages grew into cities that the local supply and demand vanished. The settlers had to go farther into remote places. By the 1830s, the vast forests of Maine, New Hampshire, New York, and Pennsylvania had been exploited on such a scale to supply the demands of urban centers on the seaboard. Thus, an important lumber industry was born.

A huge tidal wave of immigrants reached the treeless prairies of Illinois and worked across the plains west of the Mississippi River. This created a great demand for lumber that had never been seen in America before. Great areas of the plains were extremely fertile, offering farmers a rare opportunity to create rich farmlands out of the wilderness without the usual backbreaking work of clearing the land. However, the downside to that is the farmers did not have the wood needed for his buildings. The good thing is, it was not hard to get the necessary wood. Some of the forests were connected with easy access to waterways that stretches across Northern Michigan, Wisconsin, and Minnesota.

These woodlands were the basic prosperity of the Great Lakes States for more than half a century. Beginning in Eastern Canada and the New England States and stretching as far west and south to roughly Lake Erie, Northern Michigan, Wisconsin, and Minnesota, and finally tapering off in a northeasterly direction into Western Canada. In Wisconsin, the real forest lay almost entirely north of Manitowoc to Portage and then to the falls of St. Croix River. In the early years of logging, the lumberman were only interested in the white pine of Wisconsin. This wood is light and easy to work with. It is ideal for all building purposes because of it being lightweight and thus is easily floated down the rivers. The glaciers not only pulverized the soil and rocks into sand, and this in turn made for perfect growing soil for the pine trees to thrive, but also carved out many lakes that were ideal for the storage of the lumber. It also provided streams so that the lumberman could float the logs downstream.

Sawmills

In 1831, two men by the names of Farnsworth and Bush saw that the fur trade was dwindling down to nothing, and they wondered what they could do to keep the economy going. They saw the great possibilities of building and operating lumber mills and gristmills. They both went to the Menominee Indian Tribe for permission to build sawmills on the surveyed tribal lands. Then they went to the Department of War for the same permission. Both were granted to them, and in return, the two men would saw lumber and grind grain at a reduced rate for the Menominee tribe and the US government. A dam was built, and then the mills soon followed. This water-powered mill cut sixty-eight thousand feet of lumber every day. Then in 1856, the first steam sawmill was built by the New York Lumber Company on the banks of the river in the town of Menekaunee, a few miles from Marinette, my hometown. This mill had several owners and, over the years of its existence, had many fires burning the mill to the ground, but like the phoenix rising, each time that it was burned to the ground, it was soon rebuilt, more improved than the last time. Fire was the main hazard of the early days of sawmills with almost every mill being burned down at one time or another. Before I was born, there were twenty-two sawmills on the river with nine of them on the Marinette side of the river.

My father was a Canadian logger who had come down into the state of Wisconsin and settled in the town of Marinette. This is where he met and married my mother. Together they had six children, but only three of us survived. I was born on January 5, 1897. I have to admit that I was a smart little bugger in that I could read before I went to first grade. All through school, I was able to read a book once and then relate it back to someone word for word. I had a good memory, and it helped me in school a lot. I was often exempt from taking the final exams due to my high grades in all my classes. Out of the forty-eight students, I usually was the only one with the correct answers. Sometimes they called me the teacher's pet, but that didn't bother me for I was there to get an education. I only went to school through the eighth grade. If I would have gone on to high school and college, my life might have turned out differently, but I didn't have the chance because my father wanted me to start working so that I could start paying back some of the money he spent on raising me. He didn't know any better. I didn't want to work at the sawmills in Marinette because the wages were so cheap, so I either walked or rode my bike the five miles roundtrip to one of the mills between the towns of Marinette and Green Bay.

In Marinette, there were two brothers that owned many of the sawmills in town. In my opinion, they could have paid more than a $1.10 a day in wages, but the thing was, they were out to make their own money, and they didn't care how they made it. I feel that was the problem. They paid starvation wages. Due to the fact that the people couldn't make a decent living, there were more days than money at the end of the paycheck. Because of this, the people had to charge their necessary needs at the stores and thus the saying "they owed their soul to the company store" became a reality for some people. The mill owners would not let other businesses come into town and set up shop. Many automobile factories tried to come into Marinette because of the good lake port and a good railroad center. Henry Ford was one of them that tried and failed to get past the high astronomical land prices.

Strikes

During the late 1800s and early 1900s, there were many labor strikes started by the labor force to create more humane working conditions and hours. Women, men, and yes, even children fought hard battles to create what is now a livable wage, shorter working hours and better working conditions. A great example of a strike that worked was in 1914 when the Ford Motor Company raised its basic wage from $2.50 per a nine-hour day to $5.00 for an eight-hour day. The part that is really not told are the strings attached to this $5.00 a day wage that Henry Ford required of his workers in order to obtain this rate.

On July 7, 1912, the striking members of the Brotherhood of Timber Workers and their supporters were involved in an armed confrontation with the Galloway Lumber Company and supporters in what is known as the Grabow Riot, which resulted in four deaths and forty to fifty people being injured. Way over in the Pacific Northwest in Everett, Washington, on August 19, 1916, strikebreakers were hired by Everett Mills owner Neil Jamison to attack and beat picketing strikers. The local police watched and refused to stop the brutality, claiming that the waterfront where the incident took place was Federal land and therefore outside their jurisdiction. When the picketers retaliated against the strikebreakers that evening, the local police did intervene, claiming that they had crossed the line of jurisdiction. But here in my part of Wisconsin, life moved on without incident.

I worked in a sawmill that had a paper mill in the machine room. I started at a dollar and ten cents a day. I worked two different shifts, changing every week. The day shift I worked an eleven-hour day, and the night shift I worked a thirteen-hour shift. I didn't like the switching of these two shifts because I couldn't get my body regulated. This was detrimental to my health as I was constantly feeling tired and sick more times than I care to think about. I decided that it was time for me to find a different type of work to get into. I knew that I didn't want to live in my hometown any longer nor did I ever want to work in the lumber mill again for as long as I lived. I wanted to explore and experience other places of the country. It was with this thought in mind that I decided to go to Milwaukee and go to work in the steel mills.

The Steel Mills

Back about the time I was born, Milwaukee, Wisconsin, was beginning to lose the wheat market that it had to Minneapolis and St. Paul, Minnesota. Milwaukee had been the major shipping port up until then. By the mid 1880s, the decline was so great that if the city had no other industries to pick up the slack, there might have struggle something terrible. Some of the industries that were already in place were the meatpacking plants, the tanneries, breweries, and the flour mills. However, the manufacturing of iron and steel were to become the dominant industry that took the place of the wheat.

The Milwaukee Iron Company became one of the largest industries in the city. Iron ore deposits were discovered in Dodge County in the 1840s. The Milwaukee Iron Company opened its doors at the time iron ore was discovered. To say that this was an enormous company is an understatement for it employed well over a thousand people in the 1840s. One of the things that it made was the rails for the railroads. When I was hired on at this company, my first job was to work in the yard, otherwise known today as a flunky around the outside of the factory. I did all right there, earning two dollars and a quarter for a ten-hour day, which by my recollections was better than my hometown wages per day.

The working conditions were primitive and generally unsatisfactory to all who worked there. While I was working there, the workers inside the factory joined the union to see if they could improve the poor working conditions. The company wanted to hold out for a ten-hour day, and the workers and union demanded an eight-hour day. Most of the steel factory owners resisted the change for shorter days at the same wage. Change was coming whether the owners wanted it or not. However, there was a high price to pay for those who bucked the system. I want to tell you about a few examples of what took place around the country of those who fought for justice for the workers.

In January–March of 1912, in Lawrence, Massachusetts, the textile strike is credited with the invention of the moving picket line, which was thought of to keep the strikers from being arrested for loitering. This strike is also famously known as the Bread and Roses Strike.

On September 7, 1916, in the US, the federal employees won the right to receive Worker's compensation insurance.

In 1917, Rose Schneiderman makes regular trips to the state capital of New York to lobby the legislature for the passage of a law that is twofold. First, a forty-eight-hour week for women, and second, demanded a minimum wage that would benefit the men as well as the women so that the employers would be less likely to replace men workers for lower-paid women workers.

In Canada, on July 27, 1918, the United Mine Workers organizer Ginger Goodwin was shot by a hired private policeman close to Cumberland, British Columbia, and in Brackenridge, Pennsylvania, United Mine Workers organizer Fannie Sellins was gunned down by company guards.

The Great Steel Strike began on September 22, 1919, and lasted until January 8, 1920. A total of 350,000 workers walked off their jobs to demand union recognition. The AFL Iron and Steel Organizing Committee called off the strike with their goals unmet.

December 22, 1919, in the United States, amid a strike for union recognition by 395,000 steelworkers, (that was unsuccessful), about 250 anarchist, communists, and labor agitators were deported to Russia, marking the beginning of the so-called Red Scare.

My employer held onto the ten-hour day until, well, after I had quit. A bit later on in time, I moved up to working on piecework. The piecework that I did was that of making railroad tracks. Financially, I did quite a bit better, but the wages varied from piecework to piecework in that some paid better than others. I could make as much as twelve dollars a day. That seemed like a lot of money, but it was hard work and dangerous too. It was the same old program of work schedules with one weekday and the next weeknights. I wished that the labor unions had won out while I was still there. Because of the difficult and harsh working conditions, I wonder if that is why I feel my age today.

In the summertime, we workers were required to work in heat that was 110–120 degrees. In the wintertime, it wasn't so bad, but still it was very hot to work in. I quit that job because of my eyes. I would get steel shavings in my eyes. Even though I took every precaution there was to take, including the wearing of goggles, the steel scale would fly off the bullet when you put it through the rollers. No matter what I did to protect my eyes, the steel would still get in them. Another protective gear that we wore was leather gloves. I would get a new pair about every four or five days. The handles of the tongs would get so hot that I had to dip them in the water to handle that white-hot steel. It was such dangerous work that I venture to say that if you stayed there four or five years, you would lose your eyesight. Many men did in fewer years than that.

One time, I smashed my finger, and the wound turned to blood poisoning and slowly crept all the way up my arm. I thought I had better lance it before I died from infection, so I did. When I did, the puss just flew out of my arm. It started getting better quickly after that. They did not provide medical insurance back then as they do today.

I remember there was a coworker of mine whose hat fell off his head and down into some machinery. This man, without thinking, reached out his hand and arm to retrieve the hat and instantly got his hand caught in some machinery. The man lost his arm and died the next day. I think it was very foolish of this man to go after the hat, but he did it without thinking, we all do foolish things. I know that I have done my share of foolish things in my lifetime as well. They say that's why we are called humans.

Going Out West

I had a neighbor who worked in the steel mill with me, and when I quit my job there, he said to me, "Let's go out west and work in the wheat fields of Montana. It can't be any worse than this." However, about the time we were going to go, he got an abscess on his neck. I don't know how it happened, and I really don't care. He was doctoring this abscess in Milwaukee but then came to my homeplace in Marinette. But it just was not healing up, and I wanted to go. He told me, "You better not wait for me because it's kind of indefinite as to when I will be able to go." I did go and after about three or four months, he finally was able to go too.

Some would think that I hitched a ride on a train like the hobos did around that time, but no, I didn't do that. Back when I was still in Milwaukee, one day, I found a flyer along the streets. This flyer said that the railroad company would pay your train trip to Bedouin, Montana, if you were to actually work for them. I didn't figure on taking the job, I just wanted a free train ride. They paid me five dollars just to sign up for a job plus the train ride. Chuckling, I figured that I would get off long before my destination. If I would have gone all the way to Bedouin, I would have been better off. I would have made more money, and I would not have broken my leg as I did. However, you don't know these things in advance. Later, I did investigate, but it was well after the fact.

What I found out was complicated. The Montana state legislators and the railroad companies wanted settlers to come to Montana and settle there. In what was known as the Enlarged Homestead Act of 1909. This act doubled the amount of free acres available to settlers from 160 acres up to 320 acres. In the early 1900s, the railroad companies like the Northern Railroad and the Milwaukee Railroad lines were anxious to build a customer base in the vast expanses between the East and West Coasts. The railroad companies spent millions of dollars promoting the Montana region. First, they had several agriculture display trains, and then to get the people on board the trains, they created colorful brochures like the one that I picked up off the street of Milwaukee. Then they heavily encouraged German and Scandinavian immigrants to come and embrace the new life of farming in what was advertised as the Treasure State. The growth was so huge and so fast that when the "bust" began, it wasn't noticed at all.

Unknown to me, in the spring of 1917, the rain stopped falling on Montana's northern tier. This area was one of the most heavily settled areas of the homestead era. The rain did not fall. Not a drop. Then the heat wave baked the earth to a burnt black. Add to this the grasshoppers, which came in huge dark clouds and settled on the land, stripping any living vegetation down to nothing. Now if that wasn't bad enough, let's add the cutworms, the wireworms, and the Russian thistle invasion. In addition and not to be forgotten, the wild grass fires. This was the worst catastrophe in the state of Montana's history. This was the "bust" and still the railroads brought people like me to find homesteads or to find work. Lacking food, seed, and little or no help from state relief agencies, the homesteaders left Montana even more quickly than they came. This exodus started in the fall of 1916. By the time 1919 came along, the drop in wheat prices created an even more impossible situation. So much so, that now even those who were still in the state of Montana left in droves. A sign on the side of a wagon states it well, "Twenty miles from water, Forty miles from wood, we're leaving old Montana and we're leaving for good."

To put some perspective to the drought and mass exodus of people, over one hundred thousand immigrants came into the state from 1906 to 1912. An estimated sixty-five thousand people left the state between the years of 1918 to 1925. This homestead collapse helped create a depression that would take Montana years to recover. To make matters worse, the dust bowl years of 1928 through 1938 were the driest years in the history of the state, even drier than the drought of 1917. Like I said before, the rain did not fall.

Wheat Harvest in Canada

When the train stopped in Minot, North Dakota, I got off to inquire about the harvest in Montana. The people who I stopped on the streets told me that there was a total crop failure in Montana, and that I should rethink going there. I went into the county assessor's office and asked them if this was true. They confirmed that indeed it was true. My heart sank. I had ridden all this way just to find that there was a total crop failure in Montana. What was I going to do now? The assessor suggested that I go up to Canada because the harvest up there was only half over and that I should be able to find work up there.

They told me my best bet would be to go to Regina. So I decided to head on up there. If I would have just stayed on the course that I started on, but I did not. By the time that I got to Regina, British Columbia, Canada, their harvest was half over, but the threshing season was in full swing. I walked over to the assessor's office to inquire if there were any farmers who needed help. I was told about a farmer who did need help. I went to that farmer and inquired about a job and was hired.

On the morning of September 17, I was riding one of the horses out to where the threshing crew was. The horse started bucking, trying to throw me off. I decided that there was no way that I was going to stay on that horse as she was quite set on bucking me off. I leaped, but it was more like flinging, and in the process of landing, I broke my ankle and badly shattered my leg. In today's world, otherwise known as spiral break to both my tibia and fibula. They took me by buckboard wagon to Regina to the doctor. He set my leg and ankle. However, it just did not seem to want to heal. The doctor then sent me over to Moose Jaw, Canada, as that was the nearest town that had an X-ray machine. The doctor and his nurse informed me that my leg was not healing properly because it was not set right. And in order for my leg to heal and be able to walk at all, they were going to have to rebreak my leg and then set it properly. It took all my wages to pay for the doctor's bill, and even with that, I had to write home for some money. They sent me fifty dollars. I still owed the doctor fifty dollars when I left Canada. I guess he probably thought that he would never hear from me again, but I sent him the rest of the money the next summer. It is funny how something like that can change your life forever. The breaking of my leg rather handicapped me for the rest of my life. I now walk with a limp even all these years later. In addition, even in my younger days, the cold and damp weather makes my bones ach.

I left Canada in February, which was as soon my leg was healed and strong enough to let me walk on it again. During this recuperation time, I had plenty of time to think about what I wanted to do on my next portion of my journey. It was always my intention of going down to Portland, Oregon, to work in the shipyards. Since I didn't have a free ride and very little money, I would need to get off the train at a lot of towns and work for a few days for the train fare and other necessities. The train would take me on the Canada side of the west and then drop me down into Seattle and then on down to Portland. I knew that Seattle was a logging town and that was the last thing I ever wanted to do again, so when I stopped for work, I would earn as much as I could so that I wouldn't have to stop over in Seattle. Now mind you, I have nothing against Seattle, it's just the mill work that I objected to. One of the Canadian towns that I stopped in to earn the train fare had a woolen mill in it.

The Woolen Mill in Canada

The wool mill looked pretty interesting, and I was able to get a job there. They assigned me the job of scouring the wool, which wasn't particularly a glamorous job, but it paid very well, and I could see how the wool came into the factory and left as fabric. The scouring process begins with bales of raw wool that were brought in from the sheep ranches and stored in a warehouse until needed for processing. The wool before processing is called in the grease since it is contaminated with dirt, grass, dung, dander and lanolin (grease). The purpose of processing the wool is to remove these contaminates, clean, and sort the wool in accordance to what is needed that week. This process reduces a bale of wool in the grease down to about one-third of the size of the bale into sterile wool.

When the wool arrives in the factory, it is weighed and then sorted by length, elasticity, and color of the wool. The opener, willower, and picker machines open the fibers and remove some of the vegetable matter. In the scouring mill (which is where I worked), the dung and dander are washed away and the lanolin is taken out. The wool is then sent to a carbonizing mill where it is bathed in an acid solution and then sent to a steam oven that burns the burrs and anything else that is left on the wool. Following this, heavy rollers crush the burnt matter, and the willowers and dusters remove it. The wool is then steam dried and carded and combed; then set aside for storage or is used right away. It was at this mill that I was able to earn enough money to take the train straight down to Portland.

The Columbia River and Oregon

Before breaking my leg, my intentions were to go to San Francisco and join the navy. Now with my leg shattered as bad as it was, I knew that I would never qualify for the physical exam, but I thought that maybe I could still work in the shipyards there in Portland. However, once I got there, the shipyard did not look so good to me. I went down to the waterfront along the Willamette River. It gnawed on me, it just was not appealing to me at all. You see, there was a beehive of activity going on down at the docks due to the war that was going on around the world. I could see lumber just waiting to be used for refurbishing the wrecked ships. It wasn't the water or the ships or any of the activities going on down there that bothered me, it was all the lumber that killed my interest.

As I was looking around the docks and the ships, I noticed that there were paddle-wheel boats like what you see on the Mississippi River. I walked over to the The Dalles City paddle-wheel boat and noticed that it was leaving early the next morning to go to The Dalles, Oregon. I thought about it for a bit and then bought myself a ticket. I had never ridden on one before and thought it would be kind of fun. That river ride changed the course of my life, one that I am now glad took place.

Mount Hood is about sixty-five miles east of the city of Portland and basically is in Portland's backyard. Back in 1918, Portland was a lot smaller than it is today, but it was still considered a metropolitan city. Mount Hood can be seen from any spot in the city and surrounding areas, this visibility is breathtaking beyond words. However, there was a problem, and at the time, it was a big problem. There were no substantial highway systems to get to Mount Hood, Hood River, The Dalles, and other smaller towns along the way to the Willamette Valley or even for those people to get to Portland. There was just the river and a few "cow trails" and that was it. The Columbia River is considered to be the Great River of the West. With no land roads to even consider traveling over, many families were forced to use the river to float their families and their belongings to the Willamette Valley because the best of the cow trails were just wild game and Native American pony trails.

The early wagon trains on the Oregon Trail had to come to a complete stop since the steep walls of the Oregon Cascade Mountains blocked the trail. It was at what is now known as The Dalles that the wagons had to be floated down the Columbia River to the Willamette Valley. This was dangerous because the shallow but swift water soon turned into a wild and raging river that is more than a mile wide. To make matters worse, the banks of the river are sheer walls of wet slippery basalt rocks that are as high as one hundred feet, and there are deep rapids that ran for miles.

After seeing and hearing of many of their fellow travelers losing their lives to the river, many of the emigrants realized that they couldn't navigate the waters by themselves, so they hired experienced ferryboat men to float them down the raging waters. The ferryboat men saw the chance to make a high profit and thus began exploiting the people by charging highly inflated prices to float them and their belongings down the river. Even if the emigrants could pay the high fees, there was not enough ferries to take all the people across the river. At The Dalles, the wait to get across the river was days or even weeks. This was time enough for many of the travelers to decide to stay in the location of The Dalles and travel no further, and thus a town was born. The Dalles has a rather unique way that it got its name. The French fur traders named the area The Dalles because that is the French name for basalt rock that surrounds the river. This basalt rock is also known as flagstone.

The Dalles City paddleboat's only route was to The Dalles, and then it turned around and returned to Portland. There were several other paddleboats that went to different cities along the Columbia River, but I chose this boat simply because it was leaving the docks early the very next morning.

When it departed at 7:30 a.m., I was on it. I had never seen the Columbia River before and thought it would be kind of fun to ride the paddleboat. It stopped at every town along the river to drop off and pick up freight. It felt like it took a long time to reach its destination, and it was a long trip of stops and starts. When we finally got to The Dalles, it was midnight of the following night. I stayed, and the boat turned around and headed back to Portland.

My Experiences on a Wheat Ranch

When I got off the boat, I found a room to rent for the rest of the night. All the way up the river, I was contemplating what I wanted to do next for a living. It didn't take me long to decide that I wanted to work on a ranch again. Even though getting bucked off a horse would stop many a man from doing that work again, I rather liked it, it seemed to suit me well. The next morning after breakfast, I decided to head over to the county assessor's office to see if there were any ranchers that needed a hired hand. The fella in the assessor's office told me about a rancher who needed help and told me where to go to find the ranch. I was hired, but after about two months, the rancher ran out of money and had to let me go. I wasn't too worried for I knew that I could go back to the county assessor's and find another rancher who needed a hired hand. He did know about another rancher who needed help. They ran large herds of cattle besides raising wheat and hay. It was at this ranch that I tipped over the hay wagon.

I was driving one of the two-header wagons. The header wagon has a high sidewall and a lower sidewall. The lower sidewall is where the men with pitchforks would walk on the ground beside the wagon and throw the hay up on the wagon. The higher side is so that when the hay is tossed up on the wagon, the hay falls down into the bed and not on the ground on the other side of the wagon. When the wagon is full, it takes a team of four horses to pull it. We put the two stronger in front to do most of the heavy pulling and the weaker horses behind them. To help hold the horses in place, when we get up to do some work, we take a two-by-four or a two-by-six and hammer nails into the board evenly spaced out. Then when we want the horses to stay put, we wrap the reigns around the nails, and the horses stand still until we are ready to have them move again. This board is called a Jacob's staff.

That particular morning, the farmer wanted me to include the Shire stallion in my team of horses that day. He had been lame, and it was now time to exercise him. I put him in the front on the left side. He was pretty close to a ton and by far larger than the rest of the horses. As I hooked him up, I thought to myself, *This is going to be an interesting day*. Then we went to work. I had three spike pitchers, and we were just about finished with the entire hay load. Then someone yelled to me, "Hey, you forgot those two shocks [piles of lose hay] back there." I turned around to look and sure enough, I had forgotten them. I hesitated to turn back to get them because of the load I already had on the wagon and the ground was awfully steep and the farmer had told me at the beginning of the haying season that I had better not tip over the header wagon. Then I thought about the conversation that the foreman and I had about how it was impossible for me to tip over the wagon because of the fact that the back axle base was nine- to ten-feet wide and the front axle base was the normal wagon width.

I sat there, studying the shocks, the location of the shocks, and the fullness of my load. Because of what I had been told about the axle bases and the fact that these were the last two shocks of hay out in the field, I decided to take a chance and go back and get them. It was just a little ways back, and I could do this. I turned the team around and backtracked to where the shocks were; then the haying season would be over. I stopped the team so that the spikers could fork the hay up, and I wrapped the reigns around the Jacob's staff so that I could go to the back of the wagon and level off the top of the load. However, as I was spreading the hay around, I noticed that something was going on with the stallion. Since he was on the left side of the other horses, that meant he was on the uphill side of the other horse. From up on top of the hay mound, I could see the dirt was slipping out from under his hind feet. I tried to run and reach the lines of the reigns. I was able to grab them, and I tried to start the team, but they could not be started because the stallion was heavier than the rest of them and the fact that he was on the top side of the hill. He tried to move, but as he tried, he got to slipping and sliding down. I thought, *Well, there's no use.* I picked up the pitchfork that I had been using and threw it as hard as I could in the opposite direction from where we were sliding. I figured the load was going to tip over, something just seemed to tell me to lie flat, which is exactly what I did. I flung my arms and legs as wide as I could get myself to be. The header-box went over with me under the wagon and on the ground, sliding down the hill. It knocked the wind out of me, and it took me a while to be able to catch my breath again. I couldn't talk, but I could hear some of the fellas say, "I bet he's killed," and "I think he's dead." I tried to holler, but the fact that the breath was knocked out of me and the heaviness of hay and wagon on top of me muffed what little voice I had in me.

They had to tear a hole in the floor of the header-box to get me out. The hole that they made was about three feet wide. Then they got enough hay dug away so that I could crawl out. My face was pretty scratched up because of being dragged on the ground. The spike-pitchers ran hard to get ahold of the horses so that they would not run away. They brought the horses back to the upside-down wagon. We inspected the horses and saw that the tie-in horse got a cut of about eight inches on his rump. A few other horses got hurt too but not too bad. The stallion got a cut on his rump. We did not work him again until he was healed up completely. The men and I walked the horses back to the farmhouse that was about a mile away from where this all happened.

An Ordinary Man During The Extraordinary Time

The crew was afraid that the farmer was going to fire me that day. They all stood around me and declared that if he did, they were all going to quit too. I guess the farmer knew that they were all serious for he did not say one word to me. He didn't like what had happened because I had done what he had directed me not to do, and it delayed things considerably, but he let it go. We didn't work out in the field for the next couple of days as we were repairing the hole in the wagon and made a new Jacob's staff. Both of these needed to be fixed before we could go back and load all that hay that had been dumped on the ground. As I reflect back on this and I tell you the story, I shudder to think that I could have been killed, but I think that someone upstairs was looking out for me.

Even with my limp, it didn't stop me from working on the ranch. Most of the work that I did was driving a team of horses. When I was harrowing the summer fallow (plowing the fields to keep the weeds out and ready for the next seed planting), I rode a saddle pony that was right behind the harrow so that I could ride while driving a team of eight horses. Occasionally, if I got off the pony to see about something, the pony would wander off. I was in a dilemma because if I left the team to go get the pony, then the team would know that I was gone, and they would run off. I think that the pony was wise that way. I worked on this ranch until I went into the service.

Drafted into WWI

I had to register for the draft in June. The year was 1917. They drafted me in the later part of August. My intention before I left my hometown was to head down to San Francisco and join the navy. But that was before my leg was shattered. Now that the leg is bum, I knew that I couldn't pass the physical exam. The navy's physical exam was a lot stricter than the army's, so I gave up on the navy. I didn't even think that the army would take me because of my leg. But they did. They were taking cripples now as to where before they were particular as to whom they would let in, thinking that they could fit the cripples in somewhere or other. I was there for three months of what is known today as basic training.

Mustering In

Your time did not count until you were mustered in. That is, your name is put on a list of all persons that were enrolled into the service in the armed forces. I was there a couple of weeks before I was mustered in. At first, they were not going to accept me on account of my heart. One of the doctors detected what he called a murmur on my heart. They were going to turn me down for that, but he talked it over with the other doctors, and they decided the "oh well, just let him through," so they did. They didn't hesitate about my leg, ankle, or foot.

The basic training was on the parade grounds, and they put us through military tactics with a lot of marching. They put us on one of those twelve-mile marches. Even with my bum leg, it didn't matter to them. We all had to go on the long marches, and we all had to carry sixty-five pounds of weight in a packsack during the march. I was no different from any other guy. Those marches didn't do that leg any good, and I think that because of those marches, my leg was worse off than before. There were two of those twelve-mile marches, but I wasn't going to complain about my leg because there were plenty of other men trying to get out of the service for no good reasons. I can see it all happening again as if it were just yesterday. I walked with a limp before going in the service, and I walked with a limp when I got out of the service. It was while I was in basic training when the war ended, and I was mustered out. I had to stay in the army barracks until my honorable discharge came through on December 9, 1918.

Some of the fella in my barracks were from Alaska, and I would hear them talking about life up there. It got me to thinking that maybe I should go up there and see what Alaska is all about and experience life there for myself. I spent seven years up there fur trapping fur-bearing animals and was able to come home with enough money to buy a little farm just outside of Parkdale, Oregon. When I came back from Alaska, I stayed in the town of Goldendale, Washington, for a time. This is where I met my sweetheart, Elsie.

"Well, my dear newspaper reporter, I have come to the end of this part of my life's story. I wonder, would you like to come back another time to see the letters that we wrote to each other?" She nodded her head and said, "Yes, I would love to see the letters. Thank you for telling me your story." She gathered up her things and left. I stayed by the window, looking out at the night sky. It felt good to share my experiences with someone who really wanted to know. She was interested, I could tell. I wonder how the newspaper article will turn out.

PART 2

Art and Elsie
The Courtship Years: 1927–1928

Goldendale, Washington

Elsie's hometown of Goldendale has fantastic views of Mt. Adams, Mt. Hood, Mt. St. Helens, and Mt. Rainer. To give you some perspective of the location of Goldendale in relationship to some of the locations mentioned in the letters, the town is 13 miles from the Columbia River, 70 miles from Yakima, Washington, 120 miles from Portland, Oregon, and 100 miles from the Tri-Cities and Benton City, Washington. Goldendale has always been a farming and logging community with the support of the railroads coming through to haul the harvested grains, logs, and livestock. The highway systems that accommodated Art and Elsie's automobiles took about thirty years to complete, which meant less than desirable road conditions for Art to travel on.

The downtown building that were built of wood, burned to the ground on a hot windy Sunday when almost all the townspeople were attending a picnic a few miles out of town. This fire raced from building to building until almost all the structures burned to the ground. The town stood firm and within days started the rebuilding process, only this time in bricks.

Parkdale, Oregon

Parkdale is seventy-two miles one way from Goldendale. The roads were of dirt and gravel when Art was traveling over it. Parkdale is located on the south flank of the Hood River Valley. The most prominent feature of this location is Mt. Hood. In the 1880s, trees were cut, and the forest turned into pastures for cattle. Orchards took the place of evergreen trees, and strawberry fields were planted in the meadows. The need for easy access of water was great. To water these areas, there are five tributaries of glacial sources that drain about one-third of the ice on Mt. Hood.

Hood River Strawberries

The climate of Parkdale and Hood River is perfect for growing strawberries due to the colder, frosty nights and the warm sunny days of springtime. This cold of nights and warm of days set the sugar content of the strawberries, making the Hood River Valley strawberries some of the best in the world. Many people canned strawberries back in the times of these letters. Ettersburg 121 has excellent canning qualities because of the firm fleshed berry with high color and flavor that holds up very well in canning. The Marshall variety of strawberries are also a good choice for growing as they have exceptional taste and firmness and hold up well when processed for freezing.

There is usually three to four feet in between each row, making standing or kneeling while picking the berries easier. At the end of the growing season, there are plant runners that grow. Mowing or cutting down the matted older plants, creating spaces for the new plants and thus keeping the berries at their best.

Rock Creek, Oregon
April 14, 1927

Dear Elsie,

I received your most welcomed letter this evening. I was so delighted to hear from you again. I will try to be over tomorrow night as I want to have a talk with you. Regardless of what my attitude has been towards you recently, I wish to say this: that you are one of the nicest girls I ever had the pleasure of meeting, and I would certainly be glad to hold your friendship in the future.

I hope you will not judge me too harshly when you find out the truth. Things have turned out to be so complicated with me now that I don't know what to do. I am all out to sea.

Well, Elsie dear, I know that this is a short note, but I must close for this time. I will see you Friday evening.

Your sincere friend,
Art

An Ordinary Man During The Extraordinary Time

April 21, 1927

Dearest Elsie,

I will write you a few lines to let you know I arrived here alright. I reached town about 5:30 Wednesday evening. It sure is an aggravation to drive in a slow-geared truck for that far. The only time that I made any speed was downhill.

I haven't started on my regular job yet, but they had me doing several odd jobs today. First, they had me hauling dirt with a truck, then they had me picking up lumber scraps. I want to also unload my stuff this morning before I get started hauling the dirt. There, that's done. I stored my stuff at the highway's shop as I have decided to board out of awhile, just for a change.

April 22

The work here is not altogether to my liking yet. I may like it better as I get use to everything. I am boarding at the Colonial Hotel at the present time. It seems to be a good place to stop, and it's not far from the highway shops. It's about a five-minute walk.

Do you know that when I read your last letter, it touched me so deeply that I almost cried? I have been thinking of you constantly since I last saw you, Elsie. I could not very well forget a girl like you.

The weather here was pretty decent today. I hope it continues to be that way for a while at least. I think I will drive to my place in the Hood River Valley on Saturday night. I want to see how my strawberry plants are doing. It has been some time since I have seen them. It won't be such a long drive as it was from Rock Creek.

Well, Elsie dear, I will make this short this time as I am not exactly in the mood for writing. Please excuse the pencil, I couldn't find my pen tonight. I promise to write more next time.

Lovingly yours, Art

Stevenson, Washington
April 28, 1927

My Dear Elsie,

Your nice letter came Tuesday. You wrote such a nice letter, Elsie, and it sure is a blessing to read. I want you to know that I am strong for you, and I believe that you are the one girl in all the world for me. I will try to arrange things so that I can stop by and see you on Sunday morning or forenoon as I go by.

I've been doing some thinking since I've been here. I have come to the conclusion that I am lucky to have a girlfriend like you, and from now on, I am going to endeavor to show my appreciation.

I am at my regular job, such as it is. I am running a power grader, three days a week in the valley. I heard that the cherry blossoms were frozen in the lower valley. The weather is fine for three or four days here, but the past few days, it has been rather cool. I suppose it's about the same over there where you are.

It certainly was a lovely day last Sunday. I was wishing you were along with me on my trip. Sometime in the near future, we will have to take a trip through the Hood River Valley if you wish. Sometime during the next, perhaps we can arrange for it.

I was sorry to hear of your misfortune of getting stung by a bee. I imagine it was not a very pleasant sensation, but we all get stung occasionally by bees and otherwise, such is life.

Well, dear of my dreams, if everything goes well, I will see you on Sunday. Elsie dear, I don't want you to forget me, and I sincerely hope that you will not do so. I must say good night as it is well past my bedtime.

Sincerely,
Art

Goldendale, Washington
May 2, 1927

My Dear Boy,

I hope that you are doing well and are rested from the trip to my place on Sunday. I only wished that you could have stayed longer, but I understand why you could not do so this time.

The baby chicks have started hatching, and thus far, I have forty chicks now. They are doing just fine, I only wished that I had a hundred or more. I have four more hens setting.

I attended a play that the junior class put on. It was a really good play, and I wished that you could have been with me to enjoy it with me. I know you would have enjoyed it as much as I did. It is good to do something different on occasion. It makes one appreciate life again. We have not attended a thing all winter or spring, not even a show, so my brother and I decided to attend the play for a change. We always attend the graduation exercises, so I imagine we will again this year, at least I want to. I wish you could be here for the graduation too. I guess I'm the limit, but I haven't developed the films that you took the last time you were here. I have not even finished exposing all the film, but I hope they all will turn out well when I do.

Well, sweetheart, I better close and get started with my evening chores.

Thinking of you as always,
Elsie

An Ordinary Man During The Extraordinary Time

Mt. Hood, Oregon
May 29, 1927

Dear Elsie,

I will try to write you a few lines in reply to your welcomed letter. I moved into my place Wednesday evening. I unloaded my entire batching outfit and various other articles.

I've been hoeing weeds out of the strawberry plants since I've been here. John has been helping me at it. We will exchange work with one another from now on. The weather has been very backwards here: I guess the same as everywhere else. The strawberry picking won't start for another three weeks yet, the way the plants look at present. Of course, we have to have a spell of real hot weather, then when we do, the berries will come on real fast. But until then, I have plenty of work to do beforehand.

In regards to the trip to Vancouver, I think I can arrange to make it. I could meet you folks at Hood River Saturday morning or anytime you state. I think it would be advisable to cross the river and travel the Columbia Highway down to Portland and then cross over to Vancouver, as there is a stretch of road between Skamania and Cap Horn that is under construction and is impassable. I was working down there several weeks ago, and it sure is rough. One trip over that stretch of the road would almost abuse a car.

May 30

The strawberry plants are looking better every day. I think the picking season will start about the same time as last year. Perhaps before, as the plants seem to be further advanced now, than they were at this same time last year. If there are as many berries as there are blossoms, I think I'll have to hire a truck to haul them.

How did your chicks hatch out? I wanted to set a few hens myself this spring, but I was unable to get the hens when I wanted them, and it's getting rather late now.

Well, dearest girl, I hope I get to see you next Saturday as it would do me a world of good to see and talk with you again. I must close for now as I am needing a little sleep before starting another day. Here's hoping that this finds you feeling better.

Yours with lots of love. I'll save the kisses till we meet again.

Art

An Ordinary Man During The Extraordinary Time

Parkdale, Oregon
June 11, 1927

Dear Elsie,

I will write you a hasty note while I am here in Hood River. I am figuring on starting to pick berries about Tuesday or Wednesday. So if you could arrange to come about that time, it would suite me fine. Of course, if you want to go to the picnic, you could come afterwards.

I have rented some buildings from a neighbor for housing of some of the pickers. There is a stove and bed springs in them. All a person needs is a batching outfit and blankets. You could use my cooking utensils, but it would be necessary for you to bring bedding if you want to batch and whatever things you think you will need. I think there are two women coming from Stevenson: at least they said they were. I was thinking that you could probably batch with them.

Well, Elsie dear, I will have to close for now. I hope this finds you enjoying life. Kindly let me hear from you as soon as you get this and let me know where you want me to meet you and when. I hope I see you soon.

Yours Sincerely,
Art

Parkdale, Oregon
July 15, 1927

Dear Elsie,

I think that I will be over Saturday night or Sunday morning. I expect to finish topping the plants sometime Saturday. It has taken longer than I figured because I am doing the job all alone. John was going to help me with it, but he topped six rows and got tired and decided that he couldn't stand it any longer, so he quit. It is extremely tiresome on the back and knees. I thought for a few days I would not be able to stand it myself either. But I am going strong and am topping about a half acre a day.

Are you working in the hay yet? If you are, I bet you are putting in a long day yourself.

Well, Elsie dear, I haven't much time to write this time so will close. Hoping you are well and enjoying life.

Sincerely,
Art
PS Excuse the pencil please.
"The hours I have spent with thee, dear heart,
Are as a string of pearls to me."

An Ordinary Man During The Extraordinary Time

Parkdale, Oregon
July 24, 1927

Dear Elsie,

I think it's time I am writing a few lines in reply to you. I intended to do so before this, but there doesn't seem to be much to write about as I have been staying pretty close to home.

I did drive down to Parkdale Thursday evening to listen to the fight returns. There is a radio at the garage. It came in fine from the ringside of Yankee Stadium in New York. I read in yesterday's paper that there were eighty thousand people in attendance to watch the fight. This was Dempsey's first fight since losing the world's championship to Gene Tunney a year ago in September. Though Sharkey is a great fighter, I was strongly hoping that Dempsey would win. Fortunately, Dempsey did win, and I enjoyed listening to a good fight, but boy, I sure wished I could have been there to see it in person. Maybe next time, I will bet on Dempsey and clean up on some money.

Well, sweet girl, I hope this letter finds you in good health. I will close for now. Write soon as you can.

Lovingly Yours,
Art

Boxing and the Radio

It was called the largest audience in the history. On July 2 of 1921, three hundred thousand people listened to the heavyweight boxing match between Jack Dempsey and his challenger Georges Carpentier. There were more than eighty thousand people in attendance of the fight that was held just outside of Jersey City, New Jersey. Dempsey won this fight in a four-round knockout that was scheduled to go twelve rounds. This fight was the first ever of its kind to be broadcasted to "the mass audience" with an announcer giving the blow-by-blow account of the fight from ringside. This was relayed over the new "radiophone" that reached hundreds of thousands in the United States. This blow-by-blow account of the fight by a voice that sounded loud and clear to all who heard it was history in the making.

The fight promoter Tex. Rickard saw the radio broadcast of this fight as a huge potential for his future business, and he did what he could to help along this new technology. He believed that the radio would and could be a new beginning for the post–World War I culture. Rickard created a thrown-together wooden room for the radio broadcast that was constructed under the stands. Then he had telephone lines and a radio transmitter that was brought in by the RCA Company.

At the beginning of the 1920s, the radio had been beyond the reach of the everyday people of America. A young company had started in 1916 in the cities of New York City, New York, and in Pittsburgh, Pennsylvania. It was in Pittsburgh that a Westinghouse employee by the name of Frank Conrad started sending out recorded music that was playing from a phonograph over a radio transmitter, which was set up in his garage. By 1920, Conrad's employer, Westinghouse, noticed that the broadcasts had increased the sales of radio equipment, which by way, Westinghouse was manufacturing. The company had Conrad move his transmitter from his garage up to the factory roof. Then Westinghouse applied for and was granted a government license and started the very first radio station, KDKA. This radio station broadcasted the Harding-Cox presidential election returns. The sad part is, it only reached a few thousand people.

David Sarnoff, one of the managers at American Marconi Telegraph Company, had heard some of the very early broadcasts in 1917 and wrote a memo to the Marconi president about a business proposition for development of a radio music box to sell to amateur radio hobbyists. However, his idea wasn't taken seriously because WWI was in full swing. It wasn't until January of 1920 that the Radio Corporation of

America otherwise known as RCA was founded. RCA had been formed after the US government let go of control of the wireless industry after WWI. When General Electric acquired American Marconi and David Sarnoff with it, Sarnoff wrote another memo to the president of RCA. This time, with a much more detailed proposition of the radio business and the sales of it to the American public. He later stated that he had a plan in mind for the development of a radio that would be accessible to the average household as a "household utility" much like the piano and the phonograph. His idea was to bring music into homes by way of radio. He saw a large potential market that started off with just 7 percent of the population in 1920. That 7 percent brought in a gross amount of seventy-five million dollars. The possibilities for uses were endless. But it was the broadcasting of the Dempsey-Carpentier fight that sparked public interest in the radio and helped RCA and the radio business to new heights. In fact, RCA made its broadcast debut with the July 2 1921, championship fight. And thus, even today, radio historians mark July 2, 1921, the Dempsey-Carpentier fight as a landmark event that advanced the radio era.

Parkdale, Oregon
July 30, 1927

My Dear Elsie,

I will write a few lines this morning and relate my experiences since I left you on Wednesday morning. I arrived home Thursday evening about 4:30 p.m., which isn't so bad considering what all I went through.

I drove to Centerville from your home. I didn't stop in Goldendale this time. I arrived between 7:30 and 8:00 a.m. The banker had the mule ready for me when I got there. He said that he had been looking for me the last several days. I got the mule ready and started out leading it behind the car. It didn't lead very well at first but did after I got started, that is, for the first twenty-five miles or so. Then it started hanging back. Its feet were getting sore from traveling on that fine crushed rock, and it was getting tired too.

I stopped at Lyle's for supper and gave the mule a feed of Alfalfa. After staying there for an hour and a half, I started on my way again. I went about four miles west of Lyle's, and then the mule refused to go any farther. So I stopped at a ranch along the road for the night. I got up early the next morning and started out again, but the mule refused to be led behind the car anymore. So I borrowed a bridle and some lines and drove it. The mule went along fine that way. I drove the mule to Herb's place in the lower valley and left it there. Then I walked back to get my car. I walked most of the way up and back. I got a little ride when I was almost back to where I left my car. It certainly felt good to start driving the car again after walking so far.

I didn't mind walking when I am used to it, but walking in the hot sun is not so pleasant. I drove home and rested up a bit, and I felt as if I needed a rest. John and I went after the mule yesterday forenoon and got it home shortly after noon. If I had to do it over again, I don't believe I would buy a mule that far away from home unless I could go and get it with a truck.

John had the rest of the tops cut when I got back which helped some. I've been raking the tops into windrows and will finish this afternoon. Then I will start burning them when I get through raking.

Well, it is time for me to be getting back to work, so I will close for now. I am hoping to hear from you real soon. Please excuse the uninteresting letter. I will endeavor to do better next time.

Lovingly Yours, Art

Parkdale, Oregon
August 9, 1927

My Dear Elsie,

I will now try to answer your nice interesting letter I received last week. I am a trifle slow about answering this time. But please don't think that because I don't answer promptly I am forgetting about you, for I think of you constantly. I am sorry to learn that you are not feeling very well, Elsie dear. I surely hope it doesn't develop into something serious. I am feeling first rate myself. I was in Hood River last week, and while I was there, I weighted myself. I tipped the scales at 161 1/2 pounds. I am somewhat lighter than I was, but I am heavy enough yet.

I've been working for Charles these past few days. I got through there last night and now will continue with my own work. I haven't finished my hoeing yet, and I have to apply some fertilizer to my strawberry plants. I bought 2,500 pounds of 3-8-6. It is a combination of organic compounds that build up the soil.

Thanks to the volcano eruption that have happened years ago, it has given us some of the best fertile ground for growing fruit. But I need to be mindful of the soil conditions and not let the nutrients become depleted. I do this by keeping the soil at a pH balance of between 5.5 and 6.5 for the best results. I like to use a combination of nitrogen (3), phosphorus (8), and boron (6), and then to that, I like to add a smaller quantity of lime, potassium, sulfur, and magnesium. Then on top of that, I add the straw and manure from the barnyard. All these natural compounds along with lots of rain that we get here in the Hood River Valley, and also the cold nights and warm sunny days make for strawberries that are the best, and ones that I can be proud to sell.

Time has slipped away from me, and I better get back to work. I'm looking forward to your next letter, dear.

Lovingly Yours,
Art

Parkdale, Oregon
August 17, 1927

My Dearest Elsie,

I received your nice letter this afternoon. I sat right down as soon as I could and read them, a couple of times before I folded it back into the envelope. As I go about my work, I think about the things that you wrote. I am glad you're doing fine. I've been doing pretty well.

I have worked the mule several times since I've had it, and it did better than I thought it would. For this is the first time it ever worked by itself. I believe that it's going to be a fine animal for cultivating and such like that.

Well, Elsie dear, I got my first load of lumber for the house today. I bought it at Parkdale Mill but will get the balance at Dee's Mill as I think I can get better material there for the same money. The lumber that I got today was just for the framework such as sills, joist, studding plate's girder, rafters, and sheathing.

I had a nice trip Sunday afternoon. The S family and myself took a trip up to Cloud Cap Inn. We were right up close to Mt. Hood. The elevation at the Inn is six thousand feet. Did you know that the Inn was built in the spring of 1889 (just a few years before I was born), but officially opened its doors in August of that year. A prominent Portland banker and a Colonel built the Inn after they had bought the road going up the northern slope of Mt. Hood. They also created the Mount Hood Stage Company that takes the perspective vacationers up to the Inn. The trip from Portland usually starts with a forty-mile train ride to Hood River. Then the horse-drawn stagecoach takes the travelers from Hood River up to the alpine lodge. This trip takes about five and a half hours with a lunch stop and several horse exchanges at the livery stables along the way. But we just drove up to the lodge in the S's car.

I wish you were along. I am sure that you would enjoy the views up there. Of course, we didn't see any great distance on account of the smoke from the forest fires. I want to go up there when the air is clear, and one of these days, I want to climb Mt. Hood.

In closing, I just want you to know that I am certainly thinking of you often.

Lovingly,
Art

Dee Oregon

The town of Dee was built around 1906 by the Oregon Lumber Company to serve as the company town for the mill workers and their families. The town was named after the company's vice president, Judge Thomas D. Dee. The first inhibitors of the town lived in boxcars until wooden buildings could be built due to the fact that the town was set up right along the railroad tracks. As soon as possible, there was a two-story hotel, a store, and small houses that were all located on the east side of the middle fork. Once the increased availability of vehicles and the roads improved, the workers had better choices as to where to live and thus allowing the people to get out from under the smokestacks.

In about 1910, many of the original residents of Dee Flats were mill workers. They converted the clear-cut acreage into apple and pear orchards. The town was at its highest population of 250 people between 1910 through the 1920s.

Parkdale, Oregon
August 16, 1927

My Dear Elsie,

I was more than delighted to receive your interesting and welcomed letter.

I am feeling fine these days, and I believe that I am gaining some weight. My appetite is some better than it was some time back. I am eating more than I was.

I am awfully busy these days, still working in the berry patch. It's one continual round of, well, I wouldn't call it pleasure. The work is taking longer than I figured on at first. In fact, I underestimated it by quite a lot. I didn't think the weeds would grow as they have over the last few weeks. They seem to spring up like mushrooms. There is quite a lot of white clover and grass growing right along with the plants. Pulling them out from around the plants makes the weeding a slow job. I've been bending over most of the day, pulling weeds. Lots of the weeds have gone to seed. I pull them out and put them in a bucket and dump them out at the end of each row. My back is awfully tired tonight.

John was working for Charles the past four days, but he got mad and quit this morning. The job didn't agree with him I guess.

I hardly know what to say in regards to coming over for the fair. I'm sure I won't have my work done by the time it starts. Besides, I haven't even begun to start sawing the wood that I promised S's yet. I agreed to do the wood right after I finished topping the plants, but it seems that I've been busy all the time, and I have stalled him off so long that I am ashamed of myself. I certainly would like to drive over during the fair. I am pretty sure I will for a day or two anyhow, but I can't promise to be there the day before it starts.

I am very glad you did not accept the invitation to the dance. Not that I don't want you to enjoy yourself or anything like that. But I hate to have anybody stepping out with the girl that I love. I can certainly appreciate that you didn't go.

Yours with lots of love,
Art

Parkdale, Oregon
September 7, 1927

My Dear Elsie,

I will endeavor to write a few lines in reply to your nice letter. I should have answered it before this, but I haven't been in a writing mood here of late. I will do so tonight regardless of how I feel.

I've been pretty busy since I got back this last time. I cut down the tall grass and weeds all around the berry patch and have been cutting runners of the berry plants this past week. Finally, I got through this afternoon. Sigh, I suppose that I will have to go over them again before too long as they seem to grow so fast.

I found the mule the next day after I left you, which was Monday. It was at Don's place in the lower valley about ten miles down from the Loop highway from Mt. Hood Store. It stopped there at his place to visit with some other mules as it was passing, and Don put it in the corral. I didn't have much trouble finding it. I left the mule there for Don and his boys to work as I haven't much for the mule to do at the present, and the feed in the pasture is rather short, so I thought it would be best to leave it there for a while if they could use it, Don thought they could.

I intend to start the construction of my house tomorrow if the weather permits. It seems I am getting started at it. There always seems to be something that demands attention. I will be glad when I can get my house built as I will then have a place of my own where I can hang my hat. I think I will feel more at home and more satisfied than I am at present. Batching with John is not altogether to my liking. Our ways and methods of doing things are so different that there cannot be very much harmony between us. I have tolerated a lot since I've been here, and I am getting sick and tired of it all. So I will be more than glad when the time comes when I can move in my own place of residence.

I will close hoping this finds you all good.
Yours as ever,

Parkdale, Oregon
September 11, 1927

My Dear Elsie,

It is with sadness and frustration in my heart that I write this letter to you. I really was in hopes that I would be able to present to you a diamond ring on your birthday this year. I have been planning on this present to you for such a long time. But by the way I am situated financially, I feel that I am unable to stand the pressure at this time. I really was looking forward to giving you a ring and seeing the look in your eyes and hearing you say yes. I hope you will not hold it against me that I am unable to give you one right at this moment. Please know that I am still as in love with you as I ever have been. I look forward to the future when I am able to present one to you.

After I pay for the lumber for my house, our house, and a few other things, I will be nigh broke, and the labor situation does not look at all promising around here.

The apple season will be very short. The logging job I was figuring on doing for my brother fell through as he has decided not to cut any timber. I started working on my house last week, but it has been raining so much that I have not been able to do a great deal of work on it so far.

Write when you get the time,

Yours as ever,
Art

BIRTHDAY
GREETINGS

IT IS INDEED WITH PLEASURE
THAT FOR YOU I'M WISHING HERE
THE VERY UPMOST MEASURE
OF BIRTHDAY JOY AND CHEER.

GREETINGS ON YOU'RE YOUR BIRTHDAY,
ON September 13th, 1927
Love and Kisses,
Art

Parkdale, Oregon
September 16, 1927

My Dear Elsie,

I was out in the strawberry patch when I heard a plane flying overhead, and I looked up, and I do believe that it was Charles Lindbergh's Spirit of St. Louis plane that I was watching. I read in the newspaper that Charles Lindberg flew over the Bridge of the Gods after he left the dedication ceremony for the new Portland International Airport. We drove our car over this very same bridge on the Fourth of July. That means that he flew up the Columbia River and circled around Parkdale as he was turning around to fly back to Portland, passing right over where I was. Then when I read about his flight path over this area, I knew that it was him that I was watching a few days ago.

The paper also had a chart that showed his flight courses. I was very interested to know that he flew from Salt Lake City, Utah, to Boise, Idaho. From Boise, he flew to Butte, Montana, and then to Helena, Montana. He landed in Helena. He flew over both Glacier and Yellowstone National Parks. Then back to Butte then on over to Spokane, Washington. During this flight, he flew over Anaconda and Missoula, Montana, and Wallace, Idaho. From Spokane, he flew to Seattle, Washington. On this leg of the flight, he flew over Walla Walla, Pasco, Yakima and Renton, Washington. Then he flew from Seattle to Portland via Tacoma, Ft. Lewis, Olympia,

Aberdeen, Centralia, and then down into Portland. It really is quite exciting to know that Charles Lindbergh flew over our area.

Well, my dear Elsie, I must bring this letter to a close for tonight.

Lovingly Yours,
Art

Bridge of the Gods and Charles Lindbergh

A little over a thousand years ago, the mountain on the Washington side of the Columbia River, close to what is now Cascade Locks, let go a rockslide of huge proportion as to block off a section of the Columbia River. This natural dam was high enough to back the water up as far as the prairies of Idaho. Then as nature would have it, the natural erosion of the silt and sand and dirt slowly weaken the dam and finally washed the blocked portion of the river completely away. This washing away of the blocked river allowed the water of the inland prairies of Idaho to rush down natural pathways back to the Columbia River with such volume and fury that the tearing away of even more dirt and rocks created a great tunnel, causing a natural bridge over the water. This bridge was called the Great Crossover and now, in modern days, has been renamed the Bridge of the Gods.

While Charles Lindbergh was in Paris, at the end of his thirty-three hours of flight from New York to Paris, he was contacted by Daniel Guggenheim, a multimillionaire and fly enthusiast, to see if Charles would be interested in a three-month nationwide tour and, of course, flying his *Spirit of St. Louis*. Lindbergh was most agreeable to this promotion of aviation. Lindbergh landed in forty-eight states, visited ninety-two cities, gave 147 speeches, and rode in well over a thousand miles of parades.

On September 13, 1927, Charles Lindbergh flew his *Spirit of St. Louis* from Spokane, Washington, to Seattle, Washington. It took five hours and fifteen minutes to fly this route. Then on September 14, he flew from Seattle to Portland, Oregon. Lindbergh landed on Swan Island in Portland to dedicate a new international airport. Small airplane landing strips dotted the landscape of Portland in the mid 1920s. In 1925, the city of Portland asked the Port of Portland to build the first commercial airport on seven hundred acres on Swan Island. The city wanted to increase tourism and be competitive in the international flight arenas. Construction of the Swan Island Airport wasn't fully completed until 1928. Hundreds of people lined up along the airstrip to see the *Spirit of St. Louis* fly in and to greet Charles Lindbergh.

After the Portland dedication, Lindbergh flew his *Spirit of St. Louis* up the Columbia River and passing low over the new Bridge of the Gods and headed back to Swan Island. The Columbia Gorge is a gigantic tunnel perfect for doing barnstorming and aerial acrobatics.

An Ordinary Man During The Extraordinary Time

Parkdale, Oregon
September 24, 1927

My Dearest Elsie,

I received your nice letter yesterday. It is awfully slow when one is working all by themselves at this kind of work. There are things that are so unhandy to do when there is only one of me, and I need someone else to help me lift or hold something. I've got the trusses up for the roof and now am working on the plyboard on top of that. Next, I will put the tarpaper and shingles on. Then I will have four walls and the roof up.

Today, I tripped and fell over this afternoon and skinned my shines pretty bad. Then I took a chunk out of my thumb with the handsaw. This has been the worst week I've had since working on the house. I'll have to call you to dress my wounds I think.

I did hear, by the way, of the grapevine that M. and H. are getting married. I suppose it was all decided before they each got their divorces. Their minds seem to run along those lines.

I drove to Parkdale on Thursday evening to listen to the fight returns. This time, Jack Dempsey was fighting Gene Tunney in Soldier's Field. I heard later that there were one hundred fifty thousand people in the stands. At the beginning of the fight, I had wished that I had money to bet for I would have placed all my money on Dempsey. I tell ya, it was a nail-biter of a fight. First, Tunney was down and then Dempsey was down. It looked like a sure bet of a win for Dempsey.

I'm glad that I didn't bet any money because in the end, it was Tunney that won, and Dempsey was knocked out and did not get up again. Yes, I sure am glad that I didn't bet any money. My money is hard to come by, so much so that I would not care to chance losing any of it. I've got to hang on to what little I have as winter is coming on. I haven't worked for anybody except for myself this summer, so I have no source of income at present.

Well, dear heart, I will have to close for now.

*Yours with love,
Art*

Boxing and the 1920s

The United States had a huge victory in World War 1, and the Roaring Twenties brought boxing out of the Stone Age and into popularity and sophistication with the help of the radio and motion pictures and very famous people attending these fights. But not all was a bed of roses during these fights. One cannot discount that racial discrimination kept great fighters out of the ring just because of the color of their skin and that even though Jack Johnson, the first prominent black boxer, was let in, Harry Willis was locked out.

The 1920s also brought about an end for the original eight weight classes. Title bouts at the junior lightweight and the junior welterweight began. Even though these divisions were considered to be afterthoughts (and would be considered thus for decades afterward), the importance of what came out of it was born in the 1920s. The beginning of the sport's power structure is the foundation of today's sports powerhouse.

Remember that we talked about Tex Rickard? Well, even though he was the original promoter of boxing and became the main person in these events, he was also an overtly visible, meddlesome, and a very corruptible influence. He ruled the sport with an iron fist and began the troubling trend of being the major shot caller in the sport. Not as an objective arbiter as he should have been, but rather, he and others with deep pockets felt that since they were the ones with the major financial buck behind them, they had the major financial stake in the proceedings of the boxing sport itself. They felt that they had the right to call the shots, whatever the shots were.

Joseph Cukoschay a.k.a. Jack Sharkey

Jack Sharkey was born Joseph Paul Cukoschay or sometimes interchanged with Zukauskas. He was born to Lithuanian parents who immigrated to New York then later to Boston, Massachusetts. As a teen, he tried to enlist into the First World War but was turned away due to his young age. He was able to enlist in the navy after the war was over, and it was in the navy that he showed an interest in fighting for money. By the time he was honorably discharged, he had won two fights and was being written up in *The Boston Globe*. He was a tall and husky man, and because he could outbox anyone on the ship, he was encouraged by his friends to step into the ring. It was on a brief stay in Boston that he took part in his first fight for pay.

He took the name Jack Sharkey after his two idols in the boxing world: Jack for Jack Dempsey, and Sharkey after Tom Sharkey. He won his first important fight in 1926, but his big year was in 1927 when he won the fights between himself and Mike McTigue and then Jim Maloney. Those two wins put him in the ring with Jack Dempsey in July of 1927. The winner of that match was to go on and meet heavyweight champion Gene Tunney for the heavyweight title. For six rounds, Sharkey outboxed Dempsey, who kept hitting him with below-the-belt blows. In the seventh round, Sharkey turned his head to complain to the referee about the low blows when Dempsey landed a classic left hook to Sharkey's head and knocked out Sharkey.

Sharkey has the auspicious record of fighting both Jack Dempsey and Joe Lewis (on August 18, 1936) during his career. It was said of him that he had good skills. He could hit with power, boxed well, and he could take the punishment, but he was erratic, up and down. He was a boxer who never seemed to be able to pull all his skills together for fluid consistency. It was also said of him that when he was good, he was very good, but when he was bad, he was awful. Sharkey retired in 1936. He had saved most of his money, and with that money, he bought a bar and worked as a boxing and wrestling referee in the United States and Canada. He also earned money from personal appearances and entertained the troops in Africa during WWII. He also had a passion for fly-fishing, and he toured with baseball great Ted Williams, promoting fly-fishing. He was inducted into the International Boxing Hall of Fame in 1994 and died a few months later at the age of ninety-one.

Gene Tunney- The Fighting Machine

Gene Tunney fought, for the second time, Jack Dempsey on September 22, 1927, and this fight went down in the record book as the Long Count Fight. Tunney was an extremely skilled boxer who excelled in defense and preferred watching his opponents. This waiting and watching made the boxing match a game of chess for him, and it drove his opponent to be angry. His opponents wanted the center stage, actually, they commanded the center of attention, but Tunney was always moving and boxing behind his superior left jab and always studying his opponent during the match. From the first bell to the final blow, Tunney always stayed on the outside of the ring, using quick counterattacks, which kept his opponents off-balance. He wasn't a big puncher, but he could hit with power, especially after figuring out their moves and hitting when they were hurt, hard. Tunney's style was that he kept his hands low for greater power and has a fast footwork that he could adjust to every move his opponent made. He also had a quick and dead-on, one-two style of a counterpunch with a left and a right. The only time he was knocked down was in the Long Count Fight. In 1928, Tunney was elected as the first ever fighter of the year and in 1980 elected into the World Boxing Hall of Fame. In 1990, he was elected into the International Boxing Hall of Fame and the United States Marine Corps Sports Hall of Fame. He died in 1978 at the age of eighty-one.

Jack Dempsey

Out of the top ten boxers of the 1920s, Jack Dempsey was considered to be the best and "most influential" fighter. He dominated this decade of boxing sport and became boxing's first superhero. Jack was born in 1895 in Manassas, Colorado. At age twenty-four, he became the world heavyweight champion on July 4, 1919, when he defeated Jess Willard. During his career, he defeated both George Carpentier and Luis Firpo. In 1927, he lost his title to Gene Tunney in what is known as the Long Count Fight.

The Long Count Fight

Starting with this fight, there was a new rule regarding knockouts. The fallen fighter would have ten seconds to rise to his feet under his own power after his opponent moved to a neutral corner, this being a corner with no trainer in it. This new rule, which was not yet accepted worldwide, was asked to be used in this fight by Dempsey's people. However, for whatever reason, Dempsey ignored the setting of this new rule. He was in the final days of training for the fight and was cocky. However, the fight was to be held inside a twenty-foot ring and favored the boxer's superior footwork, which in this case was Tunney. Dempsey likes to crowd his opponent, thus needing only a sixteen-foot ring. Tunney was dominating the fight from round 1 to round 6. Tunney was in his usual style of watching his opponent and looking for openings and holding his hands low. There was nothing to indicate that this fight would be any different from the last time they met.

In round seven, boxing history would change forever for these two men and the entire boxing world. Dempsey had

Tunney trapped against the ropes and near a corner. It was at this point that Dempsey unleashed a combination of punches that floored the champion. Two rights and a left landed on Tunney's chin and staggered him, then four more punches, and Tunney was on the floor. This was the first time ever that Tunney had been knocked down. Dizzy and disorientated, Tunney grabbed the top rope of the ring with his left hand. Dempsey, who used to stand over his opponents and rush at them after they got up, looked down at Tunney. The referee ordered Dempsey back into a neutral corner. But Dempsey paid no attention to the referee. He just stood there, watching Tunney. This gave Tunney the precious seconds needed for recuperation. By the time Dempsey walked to the neutral corner, Tunney had been down for eight seconds. The referee could not start the count until Dempsey reached the neutral corner. He was able to count to nine before Tunney got up.

By the eighth round, Tunney had regained his strength, and he floored Dempsey with a punch. It is notable that the referee started the count right away before Tunney had a chance to move to the neutral corner. Tunney out-boxed Dempsey the final two rounds and kept his world title by a unanimous decision. After the fight, Dempsey lifted Tunney's arm and said, "You were the best. You fought a smart fight, kid." This was Dempsey's last fight, and Tunney's next to the last fight. In 2011, Tunney's family donated the gloves that he wore in this fight to the Smithsonian's National Museum of American History.

One final note about this fight, Dempsey was one of the most unforgettable boxing characters in boxing history. In the defeat of this fight, he gained more stature. It is said of him that he was the loser in the battle of the Long Count Fight and yet the hero. Dempsey died in 1983 at the age of eighty-seven.

Parkdale, Oregon
October 4, 1927

My Dear Elsie,

Your nice letter came Friday. I've been giving the berry patch the final going over for the season. I've been cutting runners and hoeing weeds. I discontinued work on the house for a while as my cash flow is running low, and I don't want to be flat broke this time of year.

I would certainly like to come over for the Indian doings at Goldendale this week. But at the present, I am afraid that it is out of the question as I am just about financially embarrassed. I would enjoy hearing about the doings, that is if you intend on going to it.

I just received a hurried call from my brother at Camas Valley, and it looks as if it is necessary for me to go down and see what's up. I would very much like to see you again before I leave, but I don't see how I can manage it. I may not start until Monday. I don't know how long I will be gone, but I hope it's not very long. I may do some hunting and trapping while I am at my brother's. I am hoping to clean up a little money while I'm there, that is if there are any furry animals.

There can't be much of Centerville now. They have been having fire quit regularly the past year. If this keeps up, there won't be any town left. When did Centerville Bank consolidate with Pioneer Bank of Goldendale? Or do you know anything about it? I know my account was transferred some time ago, but I never received any notice to that effect. I've had my account transferred to the First National Bank in Hood River, what little I have left. I thought it may be necessary to borrow money in the future, and if I do business with the local bank, I would stand a better chance of making a loan. Of course, I don't like to borrow money if I can get away without it. But sometimes it is necessary.

No doubt, you have received my other letters by this time unless they went astray. I really intended to write sooner. Well, dear girl, I must get back to work. I surely hope this letter finds you well and happy.

Lovingly,
Art

An Ordinary Man During The Extraordinary Time

Parkdale, Oregon
October 11, 1927

My Dear Elsie,

I have not started on my trip to Camas Valley yet for several reasons. I figured on starting yesterday, but there was too much to do before I left. I will not start until Wednesday morning now.

What is the reason you don't write? It is mostly two weeks since you last wrote, and this is my second letter since I heard from you last. Perhaps you are peeved because I did not come over to see you before this. I certainly would have liked to have come, but as I said before, my money is running low, and I have to get out and earn some more. Work around here is none too plentiful, and the pay is not too good.

My brother wants me to come to his place as he thinks we can clean up on a little money there. I need money to finish the house and for various other things.

How would it be if we arranged to meet in Portland when I come back from Roseburg County? We can get married then, that is if I have the necessary funds to do so.

Did you attend the Indian doings at Goldendale last week? How was it? Tell me all about it in your next letter. Now, Elsie dear, I want you to write to me? Won't you? And more often if you please. I must go to work as I have an awful lot to do before I leave. I sincerely hope you are enjoying life.

Lovingly Yours,
Art

PS
My address will be: Camas Valley, Oregon
Regardless of what happens, Elsie, remember that I am for you Strong.

Camas Valley, Oregon
October 16, 1927

Dearest Elsie,

I arrived here Thursday evening ok and found my brother without much trouble. But he sure lives in an out of the way place and it certainly is a hard climb to get there. His living conditions are not to my liking. As soon as he is able to get along without my assistance, I think I will be back home as soon as I can.

I haven't heard from you for a long time Elsie. What's the matter? Wont you drop me a line and tell me how your are?

I am writing this from the station so I'll have to make this short as there is not much privacy here. Kindly let me hear from you soon, won't you Elsie dear?

Yours as ever,
Art
P.S. My address is: Box 55, Camas Valley, Oregon

Goldendale, Washington
October 15, 1927

My Dear Arthur,

I imagine it is about time that I write a few lines in reply to your very nice and always welcomed letters that I received last night and a week ago. I was delighted to hear from you.

I hadn't any idea that you would think that I was sore or peeved or something like that on account of my delay in answering. I surely am very sorry that you thought that in any way. I don't want you to think for one minute that I was sore or peeved or anything else because you had not come up before this. I realize that it is sometimes impossible to grant someone's wishes. I do understand that you must have been busy, or you would have been up. So do not think anything like that. And as far as giving you up, that was the furthest thing from my mind. Giving you up would be unquestionably next to impossible. Dear boy, sweet boy. I think of you constantly, and I dream of you at night. This is no josh either.

If you will kindly excuse my neglect, I'll try and explain my reason for delaying to answer you sooner.

You see, the last letter you received from me was mailed the same day that I received yours. So then I would wait until you answered mine before I wrote again as I wanted to tell you about the Indian Conclave. Well, then I received your reply a week ago yesterday (Friday) on my way to town to the fair. I fully intended to write then on Sunday, but when I read that you were intending to leave the next day, I knew that you would not receive my letter before you left. So I hardly knew what to do as you never gave me any address. I first thought I would write and address it to Parkdale, and they could forward it on to you. But on second thought, it occurred to me that maybe they didn't know any more about it than I did. Then I thought of sending it to Roseburg, but I knew that it was a northern lodge place. With only that much of an address, I came to the conclusion that I would wait until I heard from you again and therefore having an address in which to mail my letters to you. These are the facts of the case.

I am real glad that you are enjoying good health and hope that you continue to do so. As for myself, I have not been feeling anything extra, but I could be worse, so I'll not complain.

I suppose you arrive down there okay. Anyway, I'm hoping that you did. How did you find everything and how is your brother? Is he nervous as he was last winter? I surly hope that he is somewhat improved from then.

What have you been doing since you arrived down there?

I'm sorry that you were disappointed because we didn't drive up that way Sunday. As with you, the work does come first. We just finished yesterday. They would have finished quite a while ago if they hadn't been delayed with so much by all the rain.

We were all tired from the fair, so we just stayed at the house until after the evening chore time and then took the folks back into town for school the next day. And still another reason, we didn't use the Buick often enough to keep the battery charged and it was running down and we were unable to start it. My brother took the battery out and is going to take it to town and have it charged up again.

We kind of looking for our cousins over in Sunnyside to stop by sometime today.

I was awfully sorry that you were unable to be here to attend the Indian Conclave last week. I am sure that you would have enjoyed it. We attended the last two days (Friday and Saturday). It was almost as good as the county fair. The races were fine. The only bad feature about them, they were rather slow in getting started. There were numerous special features such as tug of war, pie-eating contest, beauty contests, costume contest, teepee contest, food-and-pie races, and more that I cannot think of. The races and special events were for Indians only. The whites had nothing to do with it whatsoever. The food-and-pie races sure were a scream to watch. We laughed until we cried.

The Indians had a really nice exhibit in the pavilion. They charged twenty-five cents admission, but it certainly was worth it. They had some very beautiful artistic work. The interpreter said that they valued the exhibit at around fifty thousand dollars. The workmanship that was put into it all was gorgeous!

Well, the folks from Sunnyside just came, so I will have to finish this letter a little later on.

Here I am again, will try and finish now. What have you been doing since you've been down there? Busy as a cranberry merchant, I suppose. I have been pretty busy lately too.

Now where was I? Oh yes! There was a real good street carnival in town during the fair. Among the many different things they had going on was an athletic show. They only had wrestling, and I know much you enjoy good boxing and wrestling matches. Ted and an Indian took them on one night. I did not go in to see, but I heard that Ted and the Indian both won.

No, there is not much of Centerville left since the fire. I think it was the twenty-eighth of August that the Centerville Bank consolidated with the Pioneer State Bank. Papa and my brother were in the bank the morning that they made the deal. So you have transferred your money to the local bank. No doubt one would stand a better chance to make a loan all right, but I am hoping that it will not be necessary for you to do so. I am running kind of low on cash myself, but I have a little of the four hundred dollars in interest, which isn't so bad. It will help out a little in case of emergencies.

Don't you think, Arthur dearest, that it would be advisable for you to drive up here upon your return from Roseburg so that we could discuss the situation and have some definite plans before we get married? Of course, it is up to you. But I think that would be the best to my opinion. What do you think?

Well, Art dear, I will sign off and get at my chores. In closing, I hope this finds you enjoying life. Also, I'm hoping to hear from you real soon. I'll write more promptly next time, I promise.

Yours as ever,
Elsie

An Ordinary Man During The Extraordinary Time

Camas Valley, Oregon
October 25, 1927

My Dear Elsie,

I received both of your letters, the last one came today. I am sorry that you're not feeling very well. As for myself, for several days now I have felt out of sorts, but I'm feeling better now.

I've been here for almost two weeks now, and this country don't look any better to me now than it did when I first came. The climate is all right, a bit damper than in Hood River country. The country isn't settled enough around here to suit me, and it's too rugged. Where my brother's homestead is, the elevation is two thousand five hundred feet and a little over a mile from the highway. The elevation at the road where we start up to the homestead is around four hundred feet. So you can see, it is a climb to get there. I've climbed lots of hills in my time, but this is the steepest climb I've ever tackled, and I don't mean maybe!

I've been working on my brother's cabin, putting it into shape to live in during the winter months. When I first came here, it was only partly built. The homestead is ten miles from the post office. There is no rural delivery so we don't get mail delivery. We manage to get our mail once or twice a week. Some difference from my place where mail gets delivered twice a day!

I have been hunting quite a little but haven't gotten any game to speak of. I had the impression that these woods were full of game. So far, I'm disappointed for I haven't seen much to speak of. Of course, there are deer in this locality, but it's hard to see them because it's so brushy. I have noticed bear signs but haven't seen any. I did set up a bear trap this afternoon. I may have one in the morning if I have any luck. I intended to do some trapping when I first came here, but the outlook doesn't look promising at all.

Another man and I got lost last week while on a hunting trip. We didn't know the lay of the land, and we lost our bearings. After tramping through the timber until along toward evening, not seeing to get anywhere, I decided to climb a tree. We made it to camp shortly afterward. I thought for a while that we would be spending the night in the woods.

I must close for now and retire as the air is getting cold.

Yours as ever,
Art
Write soon as you can.

An Ordinary Man During The Extraordinary Time

Camas Valley, Oregon
November 15, 1927

My Dear Elsie,

I received your very nice letter last Thursday and was more than glad to hear from you. I intended to write to you sooner, but every time I thought I could sit down and write, something would come along that would prevent me from doing so. My brother may go to the valley tomorrow, and I wanted to get this letter off to you as soon as I could, so I will send it with him.

I don't figure on staying here much longer. Maybe a week or ten days. I can't tell exactly now. The living conditions are not at all what they ought to be to spend a winter here. So as soon as I get things straighten out, I will be back on my place at Parkdale again.

When I first came, my intentions were to make some money this winter with logging and such. But under the condition, it would be foolish to attempt an undertaking of that kind. It would require a lot of logging equipment, which costs a lot of money, and the timber is too far from the road, and the country is very rough. So you see, it makes a losing proposition to log on such a small scale here.

I did set out a few traps but haven't had any luck. There doesn't seem to be any fur-bearing animals around this vicinity.

Did you and your brother round up the cattle yet? It must not be very pleasant to start riding after not riding for such a long time. You have my sympathy for that as I do know how that feels.

If I am lucky enough to be back home before Thanksgiving, I will be over. I want to thank you for your kind invitation. I appreciate it very much.

I am glad to hear that they are graveling the road out your way. It will be nice to have a year-round road out there after traveling in the mud every winter.

Well, dear girl, I must bring this to a close as I want to write a few lines to my folks tonight before I go to bed.

Lots of love,
Art

An Ordinary Man During The Extraordinary Time

Camas Valley, Oregon
November 28, 1927

My Dear Elsie,

Your letter reached me a few days ago.

I expect to start back sometime this week. I have some business to attend to and, after that, will be on my way to Parkdale. I thought I would be away from here long before this, but it seems there is always something to hold a fella back. I will be glad to get away from here as it has been anything but a picnic all the while I've been here. It is a poor way to start the winter, but I will get by somehow.

Jobs are awfully scarce. There seems to be a lot of unemployed men this fall. There are a lot of them traveling afoot along the main highways these days.

I am getting anxious to see you, Elsie, and I want to drive over to see you as soon as I can. I am very sorry that I was unable to come over Thanksgiving Day. I didn't have much of a dinner here. In fact, it was the worst Thanksgiving dinner I remember. We ran shy of grub just about that time. I have thought a number of times of the nice dinner I was missing by not being over there. I hope I will be in a position to accept an invitation like that next time.

There are three of us now. A new man by the name of Steinberger, he is a middle-aged man. He has been here quite a while now. Several days ago, he looked sick and seemed to be in pretty serious condition. I am going to try to get him to a doctor, but he doesn't seem to want to go to one, so it is hard to decide just what to do in his case. If he isn't any better by morning, I will take him to town. I've been taking care of him for the last day or two, but there doesn't seem to be anything that I can do to relieve him.

It sure has been a long time since we have seen each other. I hope it won't be long before we meet again. I suppose I will be at Parkdale when you write me again. At least I hope so. Well, dearest girl, I must close for now as the fire has gone out, and the cabin is getting cold and uncomfortable, so I will retire for now.

As ever,
Art

An Ordinary Man During The Extraordinary Time

Parkdale, Oregon
December 13, 1927

My Dear Elsie,

After spending over a week on the road, I finally landed home, and I will say that it seems good to be back again. Although I don't regret that I made the trip, I am poorer but wiser for having made the trip. I won't go into all the details about my experiences on the way home and during my stays in Douglas and Coos Counties. I have referred to my experiences as "my disastrous trip to Douglas County." That's the story in a nutshell.

On my way home, I contacted a bad cold and also had a bad case of poison oak. I thought that I was immune to such things, but it seems that I am not. The cold has loosened up, and the poison oak is not any worse.

What's the matter, Elsie, have you decided to quit writing me or has someone beaten my time? I thought for sure I would have a letter from you before this. In fact, I thought for sure there would have been one waiting for me when I got home. I'll have to do a little investigating, I guess. How are the roads out your way? Passable, I hope. Don't be surprised if you see me over there soon.

As ever,
Art

1928

Parkdale, Oregon
February 1, 1928

Dearest Girl,

I will try to scribble a few lines tonight in answer to your welcomed letter that I received Monday. I was pleased to get an answer so soon. I am glad that you are feeling better and are over the mumps. I am also glad that your brother is able to be around the farm now. You folks sure are having your share of the mumps. So your dad and little sister have them now. That sure is tough luck. Tell your sister that she has my sympathy.

If I had known that your dad was going to be sick, I would have stayed around and help out with the work. Sure is nice of Andrew to come and help out. No, I don't think I will take to the mumps as I am pretty sure that I had them when I was four or five years old. You seem to have plenty of work to do. You don't want to overwork yourself, dear, especially when you're not feeling extra well.

How is the weather up your way at present? It's been storming on and off lately. Rain and snow. The rain has melted and settled the snow considerably. There is about fourteen inches left. Plenty left yet.

I manage to get out most every day and do some work. I've been cutting some wood most of the time. I want to have a supply on hand for next summer and winter. I will finish cutting the tree that I am working on, and then I will overhaul my car.

Did your brother get his licenses? I sent them to him several days ago after I got home. I hope he received them all right. I went over to C's place on Sunday afternoon. I had him cut my hair. He did a pretty good job of it, better than some barbers have done. I think I will have him do my barbering hereafter. I can save that much money as he doesn't charge me anything.

I don't know of much else to write about as I haven't been off the place very much.

Write soon,
Art

Goldendale, Washington
February 8, 1928

My Dearest Art,

We are having spring here today, real sunny and warm, though it froze rather hard last night, and since it thawed out, it is awfully muddy and sloppy.

How are you these days? Fine, I hope. I am feeling fairly well except some cold, which I contracted while in town, but I am getting better since I came home and am outdoors more. I guess it was too confining in town for me. I like very much to be outside, and the weather was so disagreeable all the time that I was there. I did not get out much. I don't know what I would do if I had to stay inside all the time. I am such a lover of the outdoor life, and I always feel better when I can be outdoors.

My brother has his Ford torn down and one tire off. He is going to send it back to Montgomery Ward as he did not get the mileage he should have and it is about all shot, so he is going to try to get an adjustment on it.

What are you doing now? Still sawing trees? You don't want to work too hard, dearest. Have you overhauled your car yet? Better bring it to us, and you and my brother can overhaul both while you are at it.

I am hoping, dear boy, that this finds you in good health.

Write real soon, Art darling,
With a heart full of love,

I am as ever yours,
Elsie

An Ordinary Man During The Extraordinary Time

Parkdale, Oregon
February 12, 1928

My Dear Elsie,

I received your nice letter a few days ago, also received the pretty valentine and letter yesterday. I am glad to learn that you folks are well. I am pretty well myself.

The frost did some damage to the berry plants. It got all the blooms that were out at that time. I guess it froze here the same night that you said that it froze over there. I have most of the garden planted now. The radishes, lettuce, and onions are up already.

Some friends of mine and I went into a car dealership the other day. The dealer came over and invited us to take a ride. Of course, I wouldn't refuse anything like that, and so I got in. We went out on the Columbia River Highway for several miles. He had it up to fifty miles per hour, climbing a hill! Of course, he had to be a little careful not to exceed the speed limit. But it sure was fun to go that fast.

I am sorry that you are not feeling very well. I believe that you need a change of climate, and if everything goes well this summer, I'll see that you get a change of scenery at last.

Well, my dearest Elsie, I must close for now,
With love and kisses,
Art

Parkdale, Oregon
February 22, 1928

Dearest Sweetheart,

I am glad to hear that you are well. As for myself, I am feeling fine. I intended to write last night, but I went to bed instead. I haven't been anywhere since I've been back, so I don't know much to write. All the news that I get is what I read in the papers (The Sunday's and twice a week Spokesman-Review) and that would be stale to you.

How deep is the snow there now? I suppose there is a plenty, same as here. I hope it quits pretty soon as there is more than enough to suit me.

I have only done a half's slashing (cutting brush down with a scythe) since I got back, and now the brush is so full of snow that I won't be able to get at it until the snow goes away.

This year, I'll have about ten acres of farmland to look after. There is the six and a half acres of mine and about four acres that I am now renting from John. I will be here alone after the middle of April as John has a job up in the hills, looking after the irrigation water in the head gates. He will be up there until fall.

I finished overhauling my car last week. It seems better than it did. I got several of the valves a bit short, which makes a little noise, but that's nothing much.

Well, Elsie dear, I really can't think of much to write about, so I will close for now. Write to me soon, won't you?

With hugs and kisses,
Art

An Ordinary Man During The Extraordinary Time

Parkdale, Oregon
March 16, 1928

My Dear Elsie,

I received your welcomed letter Tuesday. On my way home from your place, I stopped at Hood River and bought some groceries, saving me an extra trip from my home to Hood River. We are having quite a lot of rain at present. It started this evening and is still at it. It froze pretty hard for several nights in a row. These hard freezes don't do the berries any good. The strawberry patch looks pretty good for this time of the year. There doesn't seem to be any sign of gophers in them. The prospects look good for a heavy crop this summer. Yes, Elsie, I am figuring on you for the ticket job. I hope you will be able to be here at that time.

I went down to Dee Lumber Mill yesterday, but they were unable to fill my order, so I made the trip for nothing. It took me a half a day to make the trip with the team and wagon. I drove over to Parkdale this morning. I made arrangements to get some lumber there. I will be able to get it by next Monday.

I haven't started plowing yet but expect to in a few days. I'm getting the equipment ready. I am sharpening the plowshares and the harrow teeth and such like that.

Do you remember that spring where we got our drinking water? I don't know if you ever were down there or not, but it is a very dangerous route to travel in the wet weather. Steinberger fell from the top rung of the ladder to the bottom and just about wrecked himself. He got several cuts on the side of his head and face and some bad bruises on his body. He is just able to walk around and that is all. He sure was a sight when he came up out of there.

I stopped at S's yesterday. The road into their place is in awful shape. It is awful rough and muddy. I asked her if she had those pictures developed. The ones she took pictures of me, but she hadn't. If she ever has them developed, and if they are good, I will send you a couple.

I bet the neighbors were surprised that Mrs. K came home. I didn't think she would myself. Perhaps the asylum would be a proper place for her.

Elsie dear, I hope that it won't be long before we can meet again. I am longing for the time when we can be together all the time instead of once in a while.

Yours with love,
Art

An Ordinary Man During The Extraordinary Time

Parkdale, Oregon
March 26, 1928

My Dear Sweetheart,

As I am not very busy today, I will try a little pen pushing. The reason I'm not busy is that it is snowing most of the forenoon and now has turned to rain. There are several inches of snow on the fields. Then with the rain on top of it all, it's pretty sloppy outside. The frost and now the snow have been hard on the strawberries this season.

I thought I didn't have any gophers, but I guess I do. I will set out some poison to kill them off. I want to cultivate the plants as soon as the ground dries off a little. If the weather is favorable, I will do it this week.

I had been doing a little farming this past week. Plowing and harrowing and picking up spuds. John didn't dig many of his spuds last fall, so I am picking them up as I plow the ground. I intend to put in a good garden this spring. I have it plowed, but the ground is now too wet to harrow. As soon as the ground dries out, I can then drag the harrow on the ground to smooth out the dirt clods and level the ground. Then I can start planting the seeds.

I bought some lumber last week and finished building the shed where the hay is in. I have plenty of stable rooms now. I brought the mule home a week ago Sunday. I also rented Andy's horse to work with the mule to do the plowing and wherever work that requires two horses. They are not a match very well for size, but they work pretty well together.

I plan on being over for Easter dinner, but I will see how it goes for gasoline and bridge fair. Oh, it's the bunk to be financially strapped again. I hate being so low on money again.

Steinberger is a lot better. He is recovering from his fall.

Elsie dearest, I will close for now. I'm hoping that you are in the best of health and that I hear from you very soon.

Yours as always,
Art

Plowing and Harrowing

The reason the farmers plows and harrows the soil is to break up the hard soil, loosening the soil so that the root systems of the seeds can grow down into the fertile soil and then grows into strong, healthy plants.

A plow is made up of a heavy iron in the shape of a curved wedge with a sharp point that digs deep into the soil. This plow, as it is called, is made for cutting into the hard ground and is pulled by horses or tractors. Then when the field is completed, a harrow is used to break up the soil up even more so that it is a fine and crumbly dirt, making it easy for seeds to grow. Harrows are also used in uprooting things like tree roots, weeds, and large rocks. One last step after seeding is that the harrow is used for covering the seeds with soil. The harrow is made up of a series of square frames with bars going across from side to side and end to end. In the middle of these bars are many teeth that are pointed down into the dirt. These frames are tied together and dragged into the ground by horses or tractors.

Parkdale, Oregon
April 4, 1928

Dear Elsie,

Will write a few lines to let you know I received your kind letter yesterday. I was more than glad to hear from you. It snowed the other day, but it melted during the day. There has been an unusual amount of rain this spring. It has been raining every day for the last month. Every once in a while, we would have a hard frost. It froze hard last night.

I haven't heard anything from Steinberger. I guess he crawled in a hole and pulled the hole in after him. I thought for sure I would have heard from him before this. Well, I have done all that I can, it's his next move.

Well, dearest, the fire has died down, and it's getting cold in here. I will retire for tonight.

Lots of love and kisses,
Art

An Ordinary Man During The Extraordinary Time

Parkdale, Oregon
April 10, 1928

My Dear Sweetheart,

I will write you a few lines tonight to let you know that I arrived home safe and sound. I got here shortly after one o'clock.

I stopped at Goldendale last night as I was having a little trouble with my car. The gas line seemed to be plugged up, and one of my tires was almost flat when I got there. I wasn't feeling extra well, so I thought I better lie over until the morning. I stayed at M's. This morning when I woke up, my voice was so hoarse that I could hardly talk. After I was up for a while, my voice got better.

Say, did your dog come back? I looked out and saw him on the running board after I passed Roy's place. I had a hard time getting him to start back home. I tried to chase him back, but he wouldn't go very far, and when I would start the car, he would jump on the running board again. So I hollered at him to go home. Finally, he turned back and started toward home. I hated treating him so rough, but it seemed there was no other way. I hope he got home all right.

I surely hope you were not offended by anything I said or did Monday. I hope you will forgive me if you were. I wish I could find the words to tell you how much I love and appreciate you, Elsie. One of these days, I hope I will be able to show you instead of trying to express myself in words. When I stop to think how far apart we are from each other, it makes me feel lonesome and blue. I hope it won't be long before we see each other again. I certainly miss you, and I am thinking of you constantly.

Lots of love,
Art

Goldendale, Washington
April 15, 1928

My Darling Boy,

I received your very welcomed letter yesterday. I was certainly delighted to hear from you again. I'm not doing much of anything today so will try and write a few lines in reply.

I was certainly sorry to learn that your cold was no better and that you were feeling so bum. But I'm hoping that your cold is much better, and you will be enjoying good health again soon. You want to be careful so that your cold does not develop into something real serious. I have been worried ever since you were here and you said that your chest was hurting. I surely hope that it is all right now. Have you regained your natural voice yet? As for myself, I am pretty well.

I am glad that you decided to stay in town that night. I was afraid that you would try and go as far as you could, and it was rather windy and chilly and since you were not feeling very well. Therefore, I'm real glad that you didn't go any farther.

Yes, dear, my dog came home that evening. I didn't know that he had gone with you. I did not come in the house immediately after you left as I went to the barn and did my chores. After my chores were finished, I didn't go into the house for over an hour. When I did go in, my little sister said that he was on the running board. You should have given him a good licking, but then I don't think you treated him half rough enough.

Yesterday was the first nice day we have had for some time now. We went to town in the morning and didn't get back home until nearly six in the evening. My brother stayed home and plowed, so I drove the car. He tuned up the Buick last Friday noon, and I drove it to the mailbox Friday and to town yesterday.

Thursday, we had another hard shower. It rained hard most all the afternoon. It also thundered and lightning some. Papa was over at R's place, and evidently, they had a good share of it too. We had another electric storm and rain showers last Monday evening.

I had to stop writing for a while and take a team of horses over to R's place for Papa. He went over to John's and got his seed drill (for planting the seeds into the ground) and had to go around the road with it, which is about twelve miles, and I took the other team of horses straight across the fields while it is only about two miles that way.

I've been trimming and hoeing the blackberries. It surely is a disagreeable job. I ought to be done as long as I have been at it, but I don't like the job so consequently am kinda slow at it. My hands are full of the briers. I s'pose you have your potatoes, garden, and etc. planted now. Have you not? My garden is coming up quite nicely now. It's been so cold that it was awfully slow in coming but will grow fast if the weather continues to be warm as there is plenty of moisture. The storm mighty near beat it back into the ground. How are the strawberry plants looking? Fine, I hope. Are they blooming yet? Mine are. Ha-ha!

Mable said to tell you that they and Barney are coming down after some berries when they ripen. Mrs. T was telling me the other day that the berries they got from you last year were some of the nicest she ever saw, and they stayed so nice and firm after they were canned. A sign of truly great strawberries.

Papa, Mamma, my little brother, and I went over to John's on Sunday afternoon. My sister went to Maryhill, must be a lot of attractions at that place as both my sister and brother go there a lot. Ha-ha!

I had better close for now and get this to the mailbox before the mailman comes. Write real soon.

Lots and lots of kisses,
Elsie

Parkdale, Oregon
April 18, 1928

Dear Elsie,

Your nice letter reached me yesterday, was more than glad to hear from you so soon. I am feeling much better now than when I wrote you last time. I hope this letter finds you feeling fine.

It seems like there ought not to be so much work on a place like this, but it seems I am always busy. If the weather had not been so disagreeable this spring, I would have had most of my work done by this time, but such as it is, I haven't. It really is too wet outside to be doing anything, so I have been splitting wood for the stove and stacked it up so that I don't have to take the time to do that at the end of an already busy day. Splitting the firewood will be one less thing that needs to be done when the weather clears up and I can start the farmwork. I have to run the ground leveler over the ground before I can sow (plant) the clover and oats, but for right now, it's too wet to do anything like that.

I hope you will pardon me for postponing my visit. It isn't that I don't want to come for there isn't anything I would rather do. I am getting anxious to see you, but I must attend to the farmwork first so that I can relax and enjoy myself when I come to visit you.

Well, Elsie darling, I must close for now and get a little shut-eye as the morning comes so soon.

Yours as ever,
Lots of love and kisses
Art

PS
Please write again soon

Parkdale, Oregon
April 30, 1928

My Darling Elsie,

I will endeavor to write a few lines tonight in reply to your nice letter I received Saturday. I was sorry to learn that you are not feeling very well. I sincerely hope you're feeling better soon.

Last Friday, I plowed some of the ground that I am going to be planting the spuds. Part of that was too wet and soft to hold up the team of horses.

Mrs. S had those pictures developed, but they did not turn out very well. But then, I couldn't complain since I wasn't the one who took the pictures.

I would like to see you more often than I do, but circumstances won't permit at present. Better days are coming, at least I hope so.

Well, dearest girl, I must sign off and get some sleep. I'll meet you tonight in the land of my dreams.

I am yours with lots of love and a kiss or two.

Art

Goldendale, Washington

My Darling Boy,

I will endeavor to write a few lines in reply to your nice letter that I received Thursday afternoon in town. I am certainly glad to hear that you have fully recovered from your cold and are enjoying good health again. I am not feeling anything extra, I was just about over my cold, but it seems like I just can't get rid of it. I have also been having a real bad headache the last few days. I had a sick headache Thursday. Gosh! I thought my head was going to burst. It hurt so hard.

My! It sure must be wet down there. Is it still that way or is it more decent? I guess we are going to have spring at last. It has been awfully nice the last three days, but before that, oh boy! Have not had any rain since I wrote last except for a light shower or two but did not amount to much. But it has been rather cool and windy.

I wish, Art dearest, that you were here today. We might go flower picking and planning our wedding. Not saying that we would actually find any flowers. Ha-ha!

Well, dearest boy, I will close for this time. Hoping to hear from you again real soon.

Lots of love and kisses,
Elsie

Parkdale, Oregon
May 8, 1928

My Dear Sweetheart,

I certainly enjoyed reading your nice letter I received yesterday. I am feeling pretty good these days, but when I get a letter from you, it makes me feel a lot better.

I was sorry to hear you are not feeling well and that your head was hurting you something terrible.

Yes, it would have been fun to go out with you, looking for flowers that have not quite come up yet. Maybe a trillium or a lamb's-tongue we could pick while making plans for the wedding.

I am on my second time over on the strawberry plants as some of them were hoed while the ground was awful wet and now, some of the weeds started growing again.

The berry plants are looking fine and are growing fast, and most of them are in bloom now. The last hard frost done some of them in, but I see where there are new flower buds coming in, so now I am not too worried.

Well, honey girl, I must sign off and get busy. There is no rest for the wicked, they say. Ha-ha!

Here's hoping we will see each other again soon,

Yours with lots of love,
Art

An Ordinary Man During The Extraordinary Time

Parkdale, Oregon
May 11, 1928

Darling Elsie,

No doubt you will be surprised to hear from me again so soon.

Well, I will tell you how it is. I took a notion to write to you a few lines this fine morning, and I didn't want to spoil a good notion, so the result is, I am doing a little scribbling.

I am still a very busy boy, I got more jobs to do than I can shake a stick ay and still the neighbors want me to help them with their work. But I had to refuse.

S were over Wednesday to get me to hoe their berry patch for them but that was out of the question. I don't suppose they liked it because I refused, but my work is just as important as theirs, I think.

I didn't get much work done at home yesterday as I went after a load of lumber for the flumes. They didn't have all the kind I wanted, so I will have to make another trip this afternoon.

The strawberries are in full bloom now. I guess the picking season will start about the same time as last year.

Let me offer a suggestion in regards to a week from this coming Sunday. Could you arrange with your brother to drive down on the Washington side of the Columbia River? Also, could you get a bunch together; I could meet you people on the other side of the bridge. We could drive down to Beacon Rock and various other points of interest down that way and spend the Sunday. It would be something different than the ordinary, and it would be a nice trip.

This is just a suggestion, of course. But if you could arrange to do so, it sure would be fine. Let me know in good time if you can make the proper arrangements so that I can know ahead of time.

Well, honey, I must sign off and get back to work.
Yours with lots of love,
Art

Beacon Rock, Washington

To describe Beacon Rock is to consider that you are looking at an 840-foot basalt rock that looks like a plug. In fact, many do describe it as an ancient volcano plug. The Missoula Floods eroded away the dirt that surrounded the rock and then eroding the softer rock material near the top of the rock. This rock is thought to be the core of a much larger rock at a place where an ancient volcano once stood.

Beacon Rock has had many names over the centuries. The Native Americans call it Che-che-op-tin. In 1841, maps listed this rock site as Castle Rock, but it was the Lewis and Clark expedition that named it Beacon Rock, and the name stuck ever since. This rock was first climbed in 1901 and became a popular rock-climbing destination. In 1915, Henry Biddle bought the rock and land around it so that they could maintain the land and the beauty and condition of the rock. He then opened it up to the public. This way, they could control the amount of roads that were previously being built haphazardly. Biddle built a trail up to the summit consisting of switchbacks and handrails and bridges and ledges. There are incredible views of the Columbia Gorge anywhere you look from up there.

Goldendale, Washington
May 14, 1928

My Dearest Art,

You surely offered a wonderful suggestion in regards to the trip to Beacon Rock and other points of interests. I have discussed it with my brother, and I am indeed very sorry to say that we could not very well make the trip on account of the durn old cows! We would have to be back before dark to do all the milking. I have a bunch of baby chicks coming off Thursday and Saturday, and I cannot very well leave them for a few days. I certainly would like to very much, and I sincerely regret that I am unable to do so.

I saw Mrs. H, and she told me to tell you that she would be unable to go down during picking season. In one sense of the word, I'm rather glad that she is not going. I'll tell you my reason when I see you again, which I hope will not be very long.

The post-office department has changed the mail schedule. It took effect yesterday. Instead of carrier coming in the morning as in previous years, he will now be coming in the afternoons. In one sense of the word, it is better, but in another sense, it isn't so good either.

Well, my darling, I need to close for now and get started with my evening chores.

I am as ever yours.
Elsie

Goldendale, Washington
May 30, 1928

My Dearest Darling Boy,

I really intended to write sooner, but I have been so busy that I just couldn't get at it. But I am writing regardless of everything else. I was past nine o'clock, and I just finished with the chores. I am rather tired this evening. My sister and I washed today, and all the spare time that I had was spent out in the garden, hoeing. My little brother is helping me. I think we can finish in a couple of days that is all except for the spud patch, which is out in the field. I have been awfully busy since you left, trying to get most of my work done, which demands immediate attention done up before I leave for Parkdale so that I will be in position to leave as soon as you come after me. I think I can be ready by Sunday if you want to come up then or any time that you want to come.

The folks are going to drive over to Prosser Washington, or rather Benton City to get my aunt, who is there visiting her daughter, this coming Sunday. They are going to make it a roundtrip.

Well, honey boy, I'm getting awfully sleepy and making all kinds of mistakes. So I'll close for this time, hoping this finds you enjoying the best of health. Please, sweetheart, write very soon.

Lots of love and kisses

Yours as always,
Elsie

PS
Anytime that you come after me, I'll try and be prepared to go.

Parkdale, Oregon
May 31, 1928

Dearest Sweetheart,

Just a few lines to let you know, I made the trip home Monday although I had a little trouble. The connecting rod bearings went haywire. They kept getting worse the farther I went, and after passing Centerville, they sounded so bad I decided to stop at Sanders and fix them. I tightened up three of the bearings, and the fourth one was just a little loose, but I couldn't get the bolt or rather the taps loose from the bolts as I only had a couple of crescent wrenches to do the work with.

I finally got it together and was on my way at one o'clock. I crossed the river at Lyle on the ferry as the bridge was closed due to the high water. I stopped at Hood River for a short time to do a little business and then continued on my way home. I arrived home late in the afternoon.

I think the berry picking will start sometime next week as there are quite a number of berries getting ripe.

The weather has been quite cold here this week so far and there has been frost the last two nights. Last night was quite heavy, and it didn't do the berries any good.

You can tell the Smith's and Brown's that they can get their berries by the ninth of June. I was wondering if you could arrange to come over with some of them as I will be terribly busy, irrigating and everything. Not that I don't want to come over and get you, and I will if there is no other way.

I got the main flume completed Tuesday, and I have got most of the berries irrigated. They don't irrigate very good on the lower end, so I put the flume in the center and let it irrigate down at the bottom end where it will do the most good.

To build the flume, I made a floor and two sidewalls with the boards together as tight as I could get them. Then I put some tar on the outside of the floor and sides so that the water would stay in the shoot and not leak out. Then I bolted tin handles onto the top of the wooden sides to be a stabilizer so that the sides would not lose their shape. Then I created a gradual downhill slope in the dirt so that the water could run at gravity pull and open slots where I wanted the water to go.

I am writing this in the morning, and I will try to get it off today so that you will get it in good time. Please let me know as soon as you can arrange to come with one of the parties I mentioned.

Here's hoping that you get here all right. Well, dear sweet girl, I must sign off and get busy as it seems my work is never done.

Lots of love,
Art

Postscript

This is where the letters stop. I too had that letdown feeling of, so what happened next? I can tell you that Art did indeed buy his Elsie that diamond ring, which he had promised to buy her as soon as he could. It was a square of small diamonds surrounding a large diamond in the center of them. They did get married in the year of 1928 although I do not know what time of year, or if it was a church wedding or a home wedding. And I wish that I could tell you that they lived happily ever after, but that only happens in fairy tales. What I can tell you is that they had their share of heartaches. One of their heartaches is that they lost an infant baby to death, and they could never have any more children. Art never really got over that lost.

I know that Art took his marriage vows very seriously, especially the part that says: "In sickness and in health, for better or for worse." For when Elsie had a stroke and Art felt that he had to put her in a nursing home for care, he would go to the nursing home every day to be with her. He once told me that he felt that she was getting less than adequate care (especially for the money spent). He said, "I didn't cotton to the way they were taking care of her, so I loaded her up in my car and took her home. I could take care of her better than they were. And I did!" He took care of her in their home for the last twenty years of her life. She died at the age of eighty-five.

I knew Art when he was in his midnineties. He was good looking even into his nineties. He was a kind and soft-spoken man. Oftentimes he reminded me of that old commercial, "When E. F. Hutton speaks, everyone listens." This was Art. He put thought into whatever it was that he felt worthy of speaking up about. And people listened to what he had to say. Art did not make it to 103, but he did make it to 102 1/2 years. I can honestly say that it was a privilege to have known this man. However, until I heard his oral history and read their letters, I would have never guessed that he lived such an adventurous life during those extraordinary times.

Rosemary Gilder

Rosemary Gilder's Bio

Rosemary was raised by her mother's parents on a small farm in Latah County, Idaho. She grew up listening to her grandpa telling stories and learned intuitively how to tell stories on her own voice. It was in this same small town that she raised her three children, who are now grown and living successful lives of their own. When she was forty-six, she enrolled in college for the first time in her life. It was while in college that she discovered her passion and talent for writing.